QUEEN

of

GLEN EYRIE

CELESTE BLACK

QUEEN

of

GLEN EYRIE

WIFE OF GENERAL WILLIAM PALMER

The Woman Who Inspired a Castle

NAVPRESS®

The Navigators is an international Christian organization. Our mission is to advance the gospel of Jesus and His kingdom into the nations through spiritual generations of laborers living and discipling among the lost. We see a vital movement of the gospel, fueled by prevailing prayer, flowing freely through relational networks and out into the nations where workers for the kingdom are next door to everywhere.

NavPress is the publishing ministry of The Navigators. The mission of NavPress is to reach, disciple, and equip people to know Christ and make Him known by publishing life-related materials that are biblically rooted and culturally relevant. Our vision is to stimulate spiritual transformation through every product we publish.

ISBN-13: 978-1-60006-311-4
ISBN-10: 1-60006-311-X

Cover design by Arvid Wallen
Cover photo from Colorado Springs Pioneers Museum

Printed in the United States of America

1 2 3 4 5 6 7 8 / 11 10 09 08

To the pioneer women
of Colorado,
the heart of the state,
and to the Colorado women
of today,
who keep that heart beating

Contents

PREFACE

The General William Jackson Palmer Historical Collection is extensive, and it is shared by several museums and libraries in Colorado. It has been carefully preserved, maintained, and organized, and it contains hundreds of important documents and personal papers pertaining to this great man. Among the collection are numerous personal letters that the general wrote to Queen that were carefully saved for posterity.

Unfortunately, few letters written by Queen Palmer to the general were saved, probably because of General Palmer's traveling lifestyle, which in the 1800s was often spartan and rugged. Also the general was a very private man and did not allow any biographical accounts of him to be written during his lifetime. If he did save the letters, he did so privately.

Most of the biographies written later about General Palmer merely skim over the part that Queen played in his life.

For this reason, other sources have been used to fill in the gaps of Queen's life. Journals, diaries, letters to her children, and descriptive accounts written by friends and acquaintances have been most useful. I wish there were more personal missives from Queen that would enable us to hear directly her thoughts and feelings. Since that is not the case, I am grateful that the other sources were available.

Celeste Black

ACKNOWLEDGMENTS

My special thanks to my husband, Tom, with all my love, for his patience and computer expertise, and to the Colorado Springs Pioneers Museum and its staff, especially Leah Davis Witherow and Kelly Murphy in the Starsmore Center, for their help and encouragement. I am also grateful to the local history department of the Pikes Peak Library; to the Stephen H. Hart Library, Colorado Historical Society; to Queen Palmer's great granddaughter, Louisa Creede and her husband, Lewis Creede, for their interest and approval; to Virginia Godfrey, Susan Veldez, and Bob and Diane Owens, for their editing talent; to Len Froisland for his generosity; and to all the others who saw the need to set the record straight and offered their encouragement!

CHAPTER ONE

THE MEETING

For the thirty-two-year-old bachelor it was unquestionably love at first sight. At age nineteen, the lovely, petite girl with the melodic mezzo voice was gentility personified. The unusual name Queen fit her perfectly.

She had just joined her father, William Proctor Mellen, in the railroad car where he was conversing with General William Jackson Palmer, whom he had just met. The general was expounding on his energetic plan to extend the railroad from Denver to Mexico City.

Queen was small and delicate, with defiantly curly hair. Palmer was a slight, wiry man, not over five feet, eight inches tall. His somewhat stern and autocratic demeanor belied his warm personality.

Somewhere between Cincinnati and St. Louis, Palmer fell head-over-heels in love.

Queen Mellen and her father were on a trip to see the west. General Palmer was on a business trip, a frequent occurrence for the director in charge of construction for the Kansas Pacific Railroad.

William Proctor Mellen, then a New York lawyer, had practiced law in Illinois and Ohio. He became supervising agent of the Treasury Department and later general agent when his former partner, Salmon P. Chase, became secretary of the United States Treasury. The year was 1869, and Mellen had recently retired to private practice and was ready for a new and exciting venture.

It didn't hurt William Palmer's romantic cause that Mellen

welcomed the opportunity to become the close business associate of this vibrant, enormously persistent man. William Jackson Palmer would become the founder of Colorado Springs.

Queen's given name was Mary Lincoln. She was born in Prestonburg, Kentucky, on March 26, 1850, the only child of Isabel and William Mellen.

When Mary was only four years old her young mother died. Isabel, the daughter of Nathan and Charlotte Ann Clark, died of "brain fever" in Lawrence County, Kentucky, at age twenty-five.

The loss of his wife must have been devastating for the young father, left with a small child to raise. We can only surmise where the nickname Queen originated, but we can assume that a lonely William Mellen lavished attention on his pretty little daughter. He later married Isabel's sister, Ellen Clark, twenty-two years his junior. Ellen and William had six more children. From the age of sixteen, Queen and her family lived in Flushing, New York.

Queen's prominent family afforded her every opportunity that a young woman of the nineteenth century could anticipate. She was well educated and modern. The beauty of her voice was recognized early and singing and voice lessons became an important part of her life. At age fifteen Queen expressed strong opinions about women's role in society in a school essay:

> It is very humiliating to a highminded woman to read the description Mrs. Browning gives in Aurora Leigh of the young ladies' education of our day. Her opinion may formerly have been a correct one but I cannot believe to be true any longer. . . . Anyone who despairs of the women of the present day, let him compare us with our grandmothers, and see if we, if thrown upon our own resources are not more capable of supporting and making ourselves useful, than the young women of that day. Where was the Florence Nightingale of their time,

to say nothing of the noble women of our own country, yes even of our own city, who have found a noble object and filled an important place in this war.

Neither do I agree . . . that women must *marry* to live, or that an intelligent man marries a woman for the sake of securing a good cook, seamstress, or nurse. *More* today than ever is a woman a companion for a man. *Less* today than ever is the term, "old maid" used as a term of reproach; for, an agreeable intelligent maiden lady has a position of her *own*, and is gladly welcomed everywhere as an acquisition to society. While the vocation of wife and mother is the most beautiful to which a woman can be called, it is not necessarily the only one, that one need be either useless or wretched to whom that calling does not come.

The nature of men and women being different, there are positions peculiarly adapted to each. A more calculating mind may fit a man better for public speaking, or heading an army, greater physical strength may make him capable of lifting great weights, but these are not the only posts of honor.

On the subject of friendship, Queen wrote:

"A true friend is a strong defence [sic] and he that hath found such a one hath found a treasure." The sentiment of *true* friendship is very rare, though it has many counterfeits, which are short lived, though very violent during their brief existence. *True friendship* is founded on respect and esteem, not for an imaginary, but for some really fine trait in each. The confidence between friends, must be entirely unlimited and unreserved. The true sentiment *acts*, more than it *talks*. . . . Between friends, there is always a strong reserved force of tenderness which is constantly making itself manifested, not in words alone but in actions. Each is always anxious and ready to sacrifice himself for the other.

At age thirty-two, William Jackson Palmer had already proved himself to be an incredible visionary.

When he was very young, Palmer's family moved from Kinsale Farm in Kent County, Delaware, to Philadelphia, Pennsylvania. There he attended a Quaker school, which contributed to the development of his strong moral character. The Quakers were known to be peace loving, thrifty, and hard working. Besides reading the Bible, Palmer liked to study the history of America. He was entranced, however, with the new DeWitt Clinton Locomotive that ran on rails at speeds up to fifteen miles an hour. From a very early age, his dream was to become a railroad man.

Toward this end he went to work at seventeen years old, surveying the land across the Allegheny Mountains where tracks were to be laid.

In an effort to learn all he could about railroading, William borrowed money to finance a trip to England to study the railroads. He was nineteen. In England he tramped from village to village, visiting iron foundries, steelworks, and railroad shops, mastering every facet of working railroads. By the time he returned to America and the railroad through the Alleghenies, the engines were burning coal instead of wood. Speeds had increased to thirty miles per hour.

William Palmer was a peace loving man. He also was a man who loathed slavery. As civil war enveloped the country, he could not remain uninvolved in spite of his Quaker upbringing. William and his friends formed a regiment, and he was chosen as captain of the Fifteenth Pennsylvania Volunteer Calvary.

He distinguished himself in the Civil War and was even imprisoned for a time in the southern prison of Castle Thunder, located near Richmond, Virginia.

He later attained the rank of Brigadier-General, becoming one of the youngest generals of the war. Palmer received the nation's highest award, the Congressional Medal of Honor, for gallantry in action. The citation reads: "Colonel William Jackson Palmer is Hereby Awarded the Medal of Honor for Actions at Red Hill, Alabama, Fourteen, January, 1865. With less than 200 men, Colonel Palmer attacked, and defeated a superior force of the enemy, capturing their field piece and about 100 prisoners without losing a single man."

After leaving the Army, General Palmer was hired by the Kansas Pacific Railroad. In 1867, he led a survey party from Salina, Kansas, to San Francisco. He covered four thousand miles, round trip, mostly on horseback, in an attempt to find the best route for the railroad to forge its way into California. It was an exciting adventure, beset by hardships and Indian attacks. He could justifiably be called a true mountaineer.

It was on this rugged trip that he became acquainted with a young English doctor, Dr. William Bell, who became a lifelong friend and coinvestor in many of Palmer's business endeavors. Dr. Bell signed on as the group's photographer, something he knew little about. He was willing to learn the intricacies of the camera in order to take part in this wild adventure. Willie Bell also introduced Palmer into English society, where Palmer made many valuable contacts.

Palmer's return trip was partly by stagecoach by way of Salt Lake City, Utah, eastward through Cheyenne, Wyoming, then south along the front range of the Rocky Mountains until he reached the Arkansas River. He continued east along its banks.

By 1869 William Palmer was the Kansas Pacific director in charge of construction to take the railroad across Kansas into Denver. The Denver Pacific Railroad offered him a similar position to close the fifty mile gap between Cheyenne and Denver. He assumed the dual job, and that breach was closed on June 17, 1870. He then threw his entire work force into completing the 170 miles of track remaining that would link Denver and Kansas City. Just two months later, on

August 15, 1870, the first Kansas Pacific passenger train chugged into Denver. The local population cheered. Denver was now connected to the "world."

CHAPTER TWO

THE COURTSHIP

Within weeks of their meeting, Queen accepted the love-struck Palmer's proposal. During a whirlwind courtship, she was swept off her feet by the dashing general. William was full of ambition and drive. He had already accomplished a great deal in his young life, but Queen was the one he was looking for to share his dreams and aspirations. Besides being attractive, charming, and especially kind, she shared his love of books, music, and plays. They also enjoyed deep, soul-searching discussions with each other, and he made her a full partner in his future plans. She found his ambition and lofty goals exciting and compelling.

William frequently visited his betrothed in Flushing, made possible by the traveling his railroad career dictated. As proper gentlemen did, General Palmer would announce himself with a calling card. One reads, "Miss Mellen, Murdock's splendid lecture comes off this evening. Will you go? I will call for you anyhow in that hope, at 7:30. Very Respectfully, William."

Another printed card is addressed "To Miss Queen Mellen with the kind regard of William J. Palmer, March 1869." It says: "Miss Mellen—An engagement prevents me from stopping—May I have the pleasure of your company this evening to Gen. Kilpatrick's lecture—on Sherman's March to the Sea." It is signed "Yours Respectfully, Wm. J. Palmer."

Queen didn't always have much notice when William came to

call. Most likely she made herself readily available when this dashing suitor was in town.

His calling card announces, "Miss Mellen—If I call in 20 minutes will you ride to the Capitol. Yours Respectfully."

It must have been exciting for the nineteen-year-old Queen to receive the one that said: "Miss Mellen, It is such a splendid afternoon. Won't you take a ride to Arlington Heights. The carriage is at the door."

They enjoyed a variety of things together: "Miss Queen, I have ascertained to my regret that the Concert is postponed until some indefinite time next week. I will call at 10:30 tomorrow AM—When if you decide (it being your day) to go to Church, I will be happy to escort you to any one you may prefer. Yours William J. Palmer."

We can only guess how some of the private humor between Queen and William originated. In the following note it is apparent that they shared special times together:

Feb. 20, 1869
Miss Mellen,
Will you grant me the pleasure of escorting you to the Inauguration Ball.

I go to Chester at noon — to see my imaginative friend, General Beale, prior to his departure for California.

I shall tell him that the grand ball play between Columbia and Washington is becoming popular — but that you are not willing to admit that the Emigrants stopped overnight at anything so unromantic as a hotel — and that on nearer inspection the turkish bath is not visible from which the Father of his Country is supposed to have just emerged.

Yours, Wm J Palmer

On one occasion he asks her forgiveness:

Miss Mellen,
I send you Mothers book—which I unwittingly omitted to leave
with you last evening. Will you have the kindness to read it today or
tomorrow, as I wish to take it with me when I go.

I also return to you "Undine and Lintram" which I have read
with great pleasure. I fear you will think I am so bad that I ought to
read the latter over again. Trusting however that your forgiveness so
generously given last evening was full and unreserved, I will not recur
to that subject.

I called on Prescott Smith this morning to see about that Blue
Ridge Cottage for you—but he was not in town. I believe I under-
stand the kind of one you want. I saw a picture of it once and it was
called "Dunkald."

If Prescott does not know of one like that, he must recommend one
as like unto it as possible in Maryland or the old Dominion. What
would you do in "Dunkald" on a day like this?

I hope they were not uneasy about you last evening. Alexandria
was rather too far for so late an hour.

I will call at 7:45 for the opera.

Yours Respectfully,
Wm. J. Palmer
March 15, 1869

"Dunkald" was a painting of an idyllic cottage in a beautiful
country setting that Queen admired. It was not long before they were
referring to their own "Dunkald." William endeavored to find the picture for her, and just in time for Christmas he was successful:

My Own Queen,
I have had the great happiness to secure for you, our favorite picture.
Here it is—all ready to hang up at our own "Dunkald," where it

will forever remind us of associations known only to ourselves, and
help to knit us, by recalling them, more closely together than ever.
Wm Christmas 1869

When apart William wrote Queen almost daily from Philadelphia,
St. Louis, and the West. It was in these letters that he shared his deepest
thoughts, concerns, and feelings. His Quaker upbringing had instilled
in him a strong sense obligation to his fellow man and a constant striv-
ing for a peaceful, ordered existence. Yet his innate pioneering spirit,
his thrill of adventure, his driving ambition, and his tireless energy
seemed at times to war against his moral convictions. He described his
quandary to Queen in his letters:

St. Louis
April 3rd, 1869

While lying in a sick bed this morning I had a serious thinking over.
I do not believe much in confessions or promises of amendment until
the result is achieved — so I will simply state the conclusions I came
to — and these very briefly — 1st. That the wickedest man in New
York was nothing to me. 2nd. That I intend to be good — My life
has been a chequered one, with all sorts of experiences among all
sorts of People — I cannot exactly say that it has been an unhappy
one, because I have been too reckless to care for consequences, or the
opinions of the people. . . . But my creed has always been better than
my practice — and hereafter I am determined that they shall be made
nearer to square — not by lowering the former but by bringing up the
latter — so that with your love I expect to attain, even in this life a
share of that positive happiness which is so different a thing from the
absence of misery, or from stoicism.

In another letter, William gently teases his lady love:

Waumega, Kansas
April 6, 1869

*It looks now as though I would be compelled to go East (sad fate!)
much sooner than I supposed when I left you. If this should prove to
be the case, shall I come and see you in Flushing — or will you be
so busy with singing teachers, etc. that it would not be an agreeable
interruption — as I have not had the pleasure of receiving a letter from
you for some time. Suppose you write and tell me what I shall do in
the contingency referred to.*

* By the way Col. S. B. Anderson is with us of whom you have
doubtless heard Mr. Parson's brother speak. He told me he had met
Mr. Parsons lately in New York since I left and that from him he had
learned "some family secrets" [the engagement]. He added that Mr.
Parsons spoke very highly of you — which I was very glad to hear,
as I did not know how you were regarded by staid and disinterested
people whom you had not had an opportunity of suborning, by being
sweet to them — and stealing away their candid judgement by looking into their eyes.*

Early in their relationship Queen learned that General Palmer
had many demands upon him. His personal life frequently had to be
preempted to accommodate his business concerns. The lack of satisfactory communication methods of the 1870s often required the
dedicated Palmer to drop everything and travel to a particular site to
personally solve pressing railroad problems. Perhaps this was an exciting part of the business world for Palmer, but for Queen it took some
adjustment.

 Raised in a proper, somewhat Victorian, atmosphere where for-
mality was the norm, Queen found it difficult to address the older and
much accomplished general in a casual, familiar way in her letters to

him. Palmer had chided her in a previous letter for addressing him formally, in her writing, by his rank and insisted that his betrothed address him by his first name. Queen proudly wrote:

Sunday — May 30th, 1869
General W. J. Palmer
No. 2. Astor House, New York, NY

My Dear Will (Am I good) You may imagine my disappoint-
ment on the receipt of your note Saturday — still, I suppose I may
as well get used to these sudden moves of yours and accept my
fate with mild resignation — I had anticipated such a pleasant
Sunday! — However — I know it was right for you to go — and
where duty interferes with pleasure, pleasure must always give way
and I shall always try to make it easy, instead of difficult as I have
done on two or three occasions, where you were so strong that I was
ashamed of my weakness — but I assure I do not intend that it shall
be so any more — My chin is not so square as yours, but it is not
very round either!

William was in Chicago, June 11, 1869, when he wrote:

Do not hesitate, my darling, to tell me how much you love me. You
cannot spoil me in that way. You would not fear to if you knew
what an inspiration it is to me — and not only an inspiration, but a
shield. Men in active life must have a thousand relations with people
that they cannot anticipate or control. They are subjected to a great
variety of temptations in consequence. . . . When next we meet, let us
take up the subject of ambition and see if we cannot get at the truth of
it. One thing I feel certain of — that amidst all the hot competition
of this American business life there is a great temptation to be a little
unscrupulous.

Queen listened to William's self-doubts with a sympathetic ear, for she recognized in him a basic goodness and found his indomitable spirit loveable.

Brief telegrams, sent through Western Union Telegraph Company, also kept the young couple in touch. Queen received a telegram in Flushing, dated June 11, 1869, from William, in Chicago, that announced, "I expect to spend Sunday afternoon in Flushing enroute to Philadelphia."

In September, Queen was in Chicago herself. William telegraphed her from Sheridan, Kansas, "I hope you have arrived safely—write me care of American House Denver until September eleventh—I leave here Monday. Wm J Palmer."

A second one was sent the same day and received by Queen at 795 Wabash Avenue, Chicago, Illinois: "Doctor Bell and I will visit you at Chicago about September twentieth if you will be there and Dr. Bell will escort you to New York if you have not otherwise arranged—answer—Wm J Palmer."

Another telegram followed to the same address, in care of her hostess, Mrs. Cooke. It continued: "We would only remain a day or two in Chicago—I expect to know today on hearing from St. Louis whether I go on to New York—do not alter your plans if they include those of Mrs. Van Cleave or others. Wm J Palmer."

Settling any plans must have been very challenging and sometimes frustrating. A following Western Union telegram states: "I am just leaving for American House Denver—answer there what you conclud [sic] upon—your dispatch not yet recd—Wm J Palmer."

By September 16, 1869, the telegraphed directive, received by Queen in Chicago says, "Just reached Denver—leave tomorrow morning direct for St. Louis—please direct letters to office there—will leave St. Louis for Chicago on twenty-first or second—I can take you to Ypsilanti if you wish to stop there—please answer here immediately—telegram will be sent after me. Wm J Palmer."

Undoubtedly Queen assumed that she and William would settle in

New York, with William working from an office in the city and Queen becoming the expected New York socialite and hostess. She had been brought up in a very genteel family, groomed to marry successfully into a similar family, doted on by her father. She was given every advantage that her prominent, wealthy family could offer. She was considered a very eligible young woman. William, however, was entranced by the West. His intention was clear when he wrote Queen:

> *Is it any wonder that — even when the Princess is left out — young men, taking the circumstances for the reality, should fall in love with a life like this, and riding year after year in this free air across these lonely plains, waging the ceaseless campaign against wild game and Indians, should finally, when they visit the East, feel lost and bewildered, like the old Frenchman who was turned out of his prison after captivity of 30 years, and who implored them to put him back.*

He was in a quandary, however, over exactly where in the West he wanted to live with his bride. In July, 1869, he saw the majestic, mystical Pikes Peak for the first time and fell hopelessly in love again. From the rusty red formations of the Garden of the Gods to the soft sage green of the prairies, he felt that this spot was worthy of his elegant Queen.

The grandeur of the Rocky Mountains never ceased to entrance General Palmer. His imagination knew no bounds. He could visualize this land as a world-renowned resort surpassing Saratoga, New York; Newport, Rhode Island; or various springs in Virginia. He thought that this wild land had the most spectacular scenery in the entire West. He shared his vision with Queen. On July 28th, 1869, he tells her:

> *My Dear Queen,*
> *After another day and night from Pueblo I reached here at 10 PM yesterday. For 120 miles from the Arkansas River we rode along the base, or not far from the base, and generally within full view of*

the Rocky Mountains. These grand old mountains — how natural
they seem and what a treat it always is to come back to them. The
night ride was by moonlight. I spread out my blankets on top of the
coach — back of a very sociable and obliging driver . . . and slept
soundly in the fresh air, until wakened by the round moon looking
steadily into my face when I found the magnificent Pike's Peak towering immediately above me at an elevation of over 14,000 ft., topped
with a little snow. I could not sleep any more with all the splendid
panorama of mountains gradually unrolling itself, as the moon faded
and the sun began to rise, but sleepy though I was, I sat up and drank
in, along with purest mountain air, the full exhilaration of that early
morning ride.

At Colorado City — 'the Garden of the Gods' we stopped to take
breakfast. I freshened up by a preliminary bath in the waters of the
'Fountain' whose valley we had followed all night and morning. Near
here are the finest springs of soda — and the most enticing scenery. I
am sure there will be a famous resort here soon after the R.Rd. reaches
Denver. The scenery is even finer South of Denver than North of it,
and besides, the grass is greener, there is more water, a little forest of
pine occasionally, and the sight is gladdened by the rude but comfortable farm-houses, which are dotted almost continuously from the
Arkansas to the Platte. If I go back the same way I shall try to stop
at the 'Garden of the Gods' and run up to the summit of Ute Pass to
take a look over into the South Park.

I somehow fancied that an exploration of the dancing little tribu-
taries of the 'Monument' or the 'Fountain' might disclose somewhere up
near to where they come leaping with delight from the cavernous wall
of the Rocky Mountains, perhaps some charming spot which might be
made a future home.

When General Palmer again returned to the valley of Monument Creek on August 7, 1869, he determined that this was his Eden. He fantasizes about their "Dunkald" home:

It is only 30 or 40 miles from the line of our Railroad on the Bijou; a good team—or blooded saddle horses—will take us across to it in four or five hours; it is also within two or three miles from the line of a Railroad that in a few years must be built from Denver Southward to the Arkansas, and so on, by the San Luis Park to Mexico; it is in a country of rich soil and most luxuriant grasses; it is close to great supplies of timber. The soil is such that the best roads in the world may be made over it everywhere with scarcely any cost, and there can never be any mud, that great drawback to country life. What shall we do with it? It is wild Government land now, waiting for someone to take hold of it and bring out its natural advantages. It seems almost finished now, so perfect is the distribution of grove and grass and rock, of hill, meadow, and slope but nevertheless every touch put to it would yield increased beauty and grace. Mr. Carr and I concluded to buy it, if it could be had, at the Government price—several thousand acres of it. And I have been dreaming ever since of how I would treat my portion of it (after you had selected it); how the Castle could be on one of the bold pine-topped hills near the mountain foot, and the farmhouses in the smooth rounded valley; how there should be fountains and lakes, and lovely drives and horse-back trails through groves—all planned and planted by ourselves—so that "Dunkald" would grow up under our own eyes, the child of our fancy and creation. How much better this would be than to find it made to our hand! And then the happiness of portioning out the deer-park, which we would stock with antelope and black-tailed deer; and the range for our buffalo, and all other animals native to the Plain, not forgetting even the agile little prairie dog. These inhabitants of the Plain, soon to disappear before the advancing tread of emigration, should here all be preserved, and with them a few Indians to recall more vividly the wild prairie life—which the Americans of a few years hence will only know from the pages of story-books. Can you imagine anything more delightful than to form and gradually to carry out, such a plan?

Nor would we be without society when we wished it. For, sharing in the grand estate should be the homes of our friends—those really our friends. No fear but they would join in, for they could find nothing more attractive perhaps in the whole range of the Rocky Mountains. And they would be glad to make their summer homes here also, here, where the air is fraught with health and vigour, and where life would be poetry—an idyll of blue sky, clear intense atmosphere, fantastic rock, dancing water, green meadow, high mountain, rugged canyon, and distant view of the kind that gives wing to the imagination and allows no foothold for it to halt upon short of infinity.

It appeared that General Palmer's energy was endless, yet he confessed to Queen how tiring his rigorous life sometimes could be. On August 22, 1869, he writes to Queen:

This is morning—and a Sunday morning too. I think I will always write to you in the morning hereafter—instead of in the evenings. It seems more natural. For after all, you are nothing but a morning-glory yourself. My little "Morning Glory"—are you not?

At night, I am fatigued and somewhat dull and rusty with all the labor and special thought of the day. Yes—I will write to you early in the morning hereafter—before breakfast, when the air is fresh and everything is bright and joyous—just like yourself, Darling.

Goodbye
Your Wm

Lake Station, November 30, 1869
What will you do when I have to make these journeys after we are married? Do you think you can stand the fatigue and exposure? I

shall not probably have to go around so much then, that is under compulsion. We will travel together a good deal though, for you are fond of it and so am I.

William Palmer had a poet's idealism. He envisioned that the town that he and Queen would build would be the opposite of the untamed, boisterous camps that usually sprang up along the rail lines. From Salina, Kansas, January 17, 1870, he writes to Queen:

I had a dream last evening while sitting in the gloaming at the car window. I mean a wide-awake dream. Shall I tell it to you? I thought how fine it would be to have a little railroad a few hundred miles in length, all under one's own control with one's friends, to have no jealousies and contests and differing policies, but to be able to carry out unimpeded and harmoniously one's views in regard to what ought and ought not to be done. In this ideal railroad all my friends should be interested, the most fitting men should be chosen for the different positions, and all would work heartedly and unitedly toward the common end . . . a host of good fellows from my regiment should occupy the various positions of inspectors, agents, clerks, conductors, brakemen, engineers, mechanics etc. for which they might be fitted. Then I would have every one of these, as well as every other employee on the Road, no matter how low his rank, interested in the stock and profits of the line—so that each and all should feel as if it were their own business and that they were adding to their store and growing more prosperous along with the Road. They should feel as if it were their own Road and not some stranger soulless corporation. How impossible would be peculation, waste, careless management on 'Our Road.'

Then I would have a nice house-car made, just convenient for you and me, with perhaps a telegraph operator and secretary, to travel up and down when business demanded, and this car should contain every convenience of living while in motion; but everything would go along so smoothly that it would not be necessary to devote a very large proportion of the time to business. About five hours each day would suffice, with ample margin for going off when desired.

It would be quite a little family, and everybody should be looked after to see that there was no distress among the workmen and their families — and schools should be put up for them, and bath-houses, and there should be libraries and lectures, and there would never be any strikes or hard feelings among the labourers toward the capitalists, for they would all be capitalists themselves in a small way, and be paid enough to enable them to save something, and those savings they should be furnished with opportunities of investing in and along the Road, so that all their interests should be the same as their employers'.

But my dream was not all of a new mode of making money, but of a model way of conjoining that with usefulness on a large scale, solving with it a good many vexed social problems.

William never doubted that Queen shared his boundless enthusiasm and love of the West. On January 30, 1870, he describes the depth of his passion:

When I rose this morning and approached the window a sight burst upon me which was worthy of God's own day. The Range, all covered with snow, arose, pure and grand, from the brown plains. As I looked I thought, 'Could one live in constant view of these grand mountains without being elevated by them into a lofty plane of thought and purpose?' And then our future home occurred to me, and I felt so happy that I would have such a wife, who was broad enough, earnest enough, wise and good and pure enough to think that a wild home amidst such scenery was preferable to a brown stone palace in a fashionable city; to go out each evening on some neighbouring hill and find each time a new vision of beauty and grandeur! How we could study each new revelation until it would become so familiar to us and so enwrapped with some little adventure or experience that

31

whenever in the future we would catch it again it would rush upon us like an old friend, recalling in a moment a whole flood of sacred associations. Could we ever live away from the mountains? Perhaps so, but I think it would always seem like exile to both of us, and that home would always feel as if it was embalmed in the shade of these grand old peaks. I feel all my former enthusiasm coming back on reaching this mountain base, which seems, after crossing the Plains, like the shore of a glorious New Land, a newer and grander and happier Columbia than that which greeted the great sailor on the beach of Santa Domingo.

Queen encouraged her husband-to-be and responded to his letters. He was happy to receive her answer. From Denver, February 4, 1870, he again tells her of his feelings:

You do not know how glad I was to find that you believe in and sympathize with my 'dream at the car window.' We will talk it over fully and have the finest sort of time when you come out, working it up in detail, but your letter has almost determined me. I have taken, indeed, a sort of preliminary step; it is so confidential yet that I hardly dare to whisper it to myself, but I have laid the smallest first flooring in the way of, or rather looking to, an organization independent of the Kansas Pacific and all other parties except my personal friends, of the North and South Railroad of which I have written to you, to go along the base of the Rocky Mountains and right past Bijou, but not near enough to make it noisy, only near enough for the cars to look graceful across the Monument Valley from our cottage. It won't hurt — when it is our own railroad, will it?

Finally the site for the country home he planned to build for Queen was secured. Originally he called it Bijou but it later was to be formally named Glen Eyrie:

On February 7th. Governor Hunt has undertaken to have Bijou surveyed and secured for me, so that it will be safe before you come out, and we can visit it together with somewhat of the feeling of possession . . . and you can scarcely imagine how happy I feel over it. I would really feel as though one of the aims of my life had failed if we had lost Bijou.

I told you about the beautiful secluded park that would make such a fine spot for a well-to-do colony of forty families. I have called it Queen's Park, after a certain Royal Creature.

Queen's first visit to the colony was fast approaching, and William wanted her to fall in love with this wild land as he had. Two thousand acres had been purchased, most of it at $1.25 per acre. Some of it was already pre-empted by settlers and investors and the holders had to be bought off. Eventually ten thousand acres were acquired, with subscriptions raised among General Palmer's friends in the East, and among the acquaintances of his old friend, Dr. Bell, in England.

Queen received a letter from William that was written March 9, 1870, from the American House in Denver:

It is just such a day as you should have for your first inspection of Monument Park and Queen's Park and of our farm. By the way, I have bought another farm in connection with Dr. Bell, Colonel Lamborn, Mr. Reiff, Capt. Colton and I hope your father also. It is 4,000 acres and lies at the junction of Monument Creek with the Fountain. It lies beautifully and is not far from the Soda Springs and the Garden of the Gods and every foot can be cultivated, and the soil is very rich. Moreover it lies along the direct line of 'our railroad' and there will be a town built on it. It is a nice spot to put about one hundred families on. It has coal on it too, and most superb grass. Do you think you can look after this colony also? It will be about nine miles from our home, a nice horseback gallop of an hour until the railway is built and then it will be much nearer. You will have plenty to do will you not, in looking after all these colonies? I wonder which will be the busiest, you or I?

It was clear to both Queen and William that she was to be a full partner in the founding of this town. She thrilled to the excitement of his visionary plans.

On a snowy day in April 1870, Queen and her father saw, for the first time, the icy glade at the north end of the Garden of the Gods that William named Queen's Canyon in her honor. The mountains stayed hidden in the gray clouds for most of her stay and the weather was miserable. Already hesitant about living in the unsettled West, Queen's fears grew when a thoughtless pioneer insisted on showing her the exact spot where two young boys had been massacred by Indians just two years before. Her trepidation was well founded because her uncle, Malcolm Clark, had been killed by Indians in Montana. William, however, was able to show her the spectacular formations of Garden of the Gods, the red rocks and green pines that would become her home, the mountains and canyons and even the antelope and buffalo that populated the plains.

Queen named the chosen home site Glen Eyrie, because of a pair of eagles who for many years had built their home in the huge rock formations high in the glen.

It was during this first visit that Queen conceived and began the drawings of their first home. The four hexagonal rooms clustered around a central chimney were Queen's unique concept perhaps borrowed from the formation of the cells of the honey bee.

The rooms on the first floor were spacious with many windows. The original plans identified some of the rooms on the second floor as "boy's room" and "girl's room," "teacher's room," and a large rectangular "school room." Obviously the young couple was looking forward to raising a family there in the beautiful glen. The third floor attic was designated as servant quarters and a small room was called the "trunk room." The basement contained a wine cellar, coal and wood storage, and a storeroom for supplies.

In *Heritage of Years*, Frances Wolcott tells about an occurrence during Queen's first visit to Colorado. A young Indian chief, leading a string of four handsome mustangs, arrived one morning. Wearing the badge of courtship, the yellow garter, he offered the ponies to Mrs. Mellen, Queen's stepmother, in exchange for the demure twenty-year-old. When his offer was refused, he retreated, resigned and disappointed, his horses trailing behind.

Queen trusted her future to William and returned to Long Island to make final arrangements for their wedding.

Her apprehension of living in the rough western frontier town was not without merit. In May a series of Indian confrontations occurred that horrified William when he realized that such a short time before he had brought his Queen through the same treacherous plains where the incidents occurred. On May 14th, he writes:

The Indians had broken out along our line west of Kit Carson and killed today some 10 or 12 of our men. To think how recently you and I rode over that same ground a few weeks ago in the moonlight.

Denver
May 15, 1870

The fighting along our line in the Big Sandy Valley continued today. A large body of Indians, reported 200, attacked a train four miles east of Lake, killing four and wounding one. . . . Our people are very much exercised, as are the people of Denver who fear the outer settlements may be attacked next.

How I rejoice that you got through the country in safety. It makes me tremble though, sometimes, when I think of the risk.

Queen's love never wavered. Her trust in William was unshakable. October 7, 1870, she writes to Palmer,

My Beloved, Only one page tonight to tell you that I am well and that I love you with all my heart — It is late — and I am very, very tired — God bless my Will — and keep him always — My prayers are all yours — My soul itself lives but for you — dear Love. Good Night — Your own little girl.

I will write a letter tomorrow. Love me, Dear. Will you? Three weeks from tonight where will we be?

Queen Palmer

(Photo courtesy of Colorado Springs Pioneers Museum)

Chapter three

The Marriage

The wedding took place in Flushing, New York. William slipped a simple, wide, gold band on his bride's finger. It was engraved, *WJP to Queen, November 8, 1870.* The day after the wedding the newlyweds sailed for Europe on their honeymoon.

The *New York Evening Post* published marriage records the following week that included the following:

> PALMER-MELLEN—At Flushing, L.I., on Tuesday evening, Nov. 8, by the Rev. Dr. Bellows, General William G. Palmer, of Colorado, to Mary L., eldest daughter of William P. Mellen, Esq., of Flushing.

The *Flushing Journal*, published in Flushing, Long Island (NY) on Saturday Morning, November 19, 1870, announced:

> Fashionable Weddings in Flushing are becoming quite frequent as the season advances. Last Saturday, General Palmer and Miss Queen Mellen were married at the residence of the bride's father in this Village, the ceremony being witnessed by a few friends. The happy pair left immediately for Europe, to visit the home of the groom's parents in England. Two approaching weddings in Quaker circles are creating a lively sensation, and will be consummated in December.

QUEEN PALMER

Queen Palmer, twenty-two years old, taken in Mexico City
during the visit she made there with her husband in 1872.

(Photo courtesy of Colorado Springs Pioneers Museum)

General William Jackson Palmer, whom Queen called Will,
was an ambitious, charismatic visionary. At thirty-two
his accomplishments were great.

(Photo courtesy of Colorado Springs Pioneers Museum)

The Flushing article does not have the correct day, and it was friends that the newlyweds planned to visit in England. The wedding, however, must have been quite a social event for the Village.

The newlyweds sailed for England on November 9, 1870, on the SS *Scotia*. A number of Fifteenth Pennsylvania officers and other friends saw them off. The sailing was smooth and uneventful. During the voyage they became acquainted with a number of fellow passengers, and their names were duly recorded, without comment, in the honeymoon journal that was a joint effort between Will and Queen. They arrived in Liverpool "after an unusually fine passage up the Irish Sea" on November 20 at 8:00 a.m. They spent the day with Dr. Bell, lunching at the Adelphi Hotel, strolling through the city streets and further sightseeing in a "delightful hansom." Later that day they continued the journey by train, reaching London at 9:30 p.m., and finding "comfortable but not elegant apartments at the Buckingham Palace Hotel, immediately opposite one of the city residences of the Queen, Buckingham Palace." A few days later they moved from the hotel to apartments at No. 10 Clarges St.

The events of each day were religiously recorded by Queen and William in their honeymoon journal. In the usual manner of the day, the journal is mainly factual, reciting names of people and places that they visited and rarely giving insight to personal feelings or observations.

The London sights included the Houses of Parliament, Westminister Abbey and Hall, which Queen described as "a wonderful, glorious old building," Hyde Park, beautiful Waterloo Bridge and other fine bridges across the Thames. Shopping, plays, operas, concerts, and musical evenings with friends, where Queen entertained listeners with her beautiful, well-trained singing voice, filled the time in London.

Often while William was involved with business meetings, Queen and Mrs. Bell called on friends and acquaintances. One day Queen and Emma Palmer went by "underground R. R." to Madame Tussaud's Waxworks.

At the end of November, the Palmers moved to the home of Dr. Bell. In the days that followed, Will frequently stayed in the city, attending to business, while Queen spent her evenings at cards, playing bezique, writing letters and reading, and going to bed early.

In the space of one week, the Bells feted the young couple with a party and three dinner parties. At every gathering, whether planned or impromptu, Queen was called on to sing. Sometimes she entertained by singing American war songs. Lively discussions with their English friends delved into the slavery question, the American war, California, and far western life in general.

The young couple delighted in an overnight stay at a three-hundred-year-old mansion, Thadenmont, seventeen miles from London, as guests of the Flemings, in a room where Queen Elizabeth had slept. The next morning William noted with interest a "revolving dumb waiter" on the breakfast table, "capital idea—Scotch." Queen taught the children of the house how to jump rope while the "gentlemen repaired to the stables and park." On their return to London, Queen went to a concert "by the finest artists in London" with Esther Bell and other ladies while "Will remained at home dining Mr. Getty."

It seemed that the three-month European honeymoon was a rehearsal of their married life—William wheeling and dealing with powerful tycoons; Queen amusing herself, enjoying music and art, sometimes with friends but frequently alone.

A few days before Christmas, Queen and Ettie (Esther) Bell "went to find a poor child to make warm. I found one boy (for whom I got a new strong pair of boots and stockings) and a little girl whom I made very comfortable with knit woolen jacket, tippet stockings, gloves, etc." That afternoon they decorated the church for Christmas, and she made note that "the eclipse took place about noon."

Queen writes on Christmas, "In the morning I found Kris Kringle had really been to my stocking for I found a beautiful watch in it! I told Will to thank Santa Claus for me, if he should ever meet him, which he promised to do." After Christmas tea, Queen read Milton's beautiful "Ode on the Nativity" to Will, and he read portions from "Paradise Lost" to her. The next day they exchanged gifts with English friends. Christmas gifts to families and friends in America had already been boxed and sent on their way.

By the end of December they moved to another friend's home, that of Mrs. Wards. There they met a number of acquaintances, among them Governor Gilpin of Colorado, a French countess, and other new friends. On December 31, after seeing a delightful play called *Ours* with "a very good actress," Marie Wilton, "we saw the poor, dear old year out, Will and I together, and welcomed the New Year in, in our usual way."

They traveled by train to Chippenham on the Great Western line, impressed that the Prince of Wales was on the train in his private carriage. They were met at the Chippenham station and driven to Dentesey House to meet friends and dress for the grand country ball. Queen wore her "white poena dress" and it was "a very pretty affair . . . We saw a great many notables, Dukes and Duchesses, without limit. I danced a good deal, and Will and I came home earlier than the others as he was not feeling very well. We reached Dentesey by half past three and went to our grand old room, the largest bedroom I ever slept in." Will departed for London the next morning and Queen attended yet another ball at the home of her hosts, the Powells, that evening, going to bed at 4:00 a.m.

In London Mrs. Palmer was fitted for a complete riding habit, including hat and gloves. Lovely black silk was purchased, to be taken to a dressmaker's, and beautiful flowers for Queen's hair, a lace handkerchief, "four months and ruin to some poor girl's eyes," and black silk dresses for Nellie Clarke, Ellen Palmer, and her stepmother, Ellen Mellen.

The couple traveled to Amsterdam and Brussels, where William met with bankers who were possible investors. Investors in London, Liverpool, and Birmingham had also been contacted. Other financial matters often required his attention.

In Amsterdam Queen visited galleries that featured Rembrandt and Rubens. She described a visit to the palace of the King, with "an obliging guide who speaks 'Franch Anglish, Dutch, anything vat you likes!' An immensely high ceiling 100 feet high. All marble, very cold but very grand, wonderful fresco by De Witt." That night they dined with friends who included Governor Gilpin.

It was in London, however that Queen visited an art exhibition with Lucy Bell and Emma Rollinson that included works by Titian, Murillo, Van Dyck, Raphael, and Correggio, "the finest collection I ever saw."

General Palmer consulted with the most knowledgeable engineers of the day in order to make the decision regarding his railway's gauge. For the mountainous country that the railroad would cover the three-foot gauge was most practical. The rails were ordered in Wales, to be shipped to America.

Early in their trip the Palmers had received an invitation to spend several days at Eversley Rectory, Wrathfield, visiting Charles Kingsley and his family. On February 7, a Tuesday, the Palmers "left London by Southwestern Railway to Winchfield, the long expected delightful visit we anticipated with the Kingsleys at last. . . . Drove to Eversley where Mr. Kingsley met us at the door and Mrs. Kingsley and Rose were waiting for us in the parlor. . . . Mr. Kingsley took me in, and we had a most interesting conversation and I went to bed feeling sure that I would *love* all of the charming family and wishing that we were to spend weeks instead of days with our new friends."

The next page has been torn from the journal, and the honeymoon odyssey ends abruptly with a brief notation from Eversley on February 11, 1871. The journal writing is picked up again three years later in Paris by Queen. The tone is one of reflection and self-analysis from a now more mature wife and mother:

Paris Feby. 3d 1875
    Four years ago we crossed the ocean, Will and I, when we began
    a journal as so many people do, thinking that we would keep it up as

long as we traveled. We have been traveling nearly constantly since, and the journal so bravely begun came long ago to an untimely and abrupt end!

Being again in a foreign country, no less interesting than England in some respects, I begin again alone not so boldly, and not with the least faith in my perseverance, a chronicle of the fact and the fancies which occur to me as we go. I do this partly for future pleasure as a reminder of pleasant or interesting hours gone by, and partly to impress more indelibly on my own mind as I go the marvelous, beautiful, often glorious works which I meet every day, very often without looking for them. There is no need, there they are, defying us in their acknowledged grace and beauty.

I have, to tell the truth, no plan in this my beginning. Perhaps I will close the book in disgust when I find how impossible it is for me to describe satisfactorily my impressions. Perhaps instead of chronicling the facts and brief impressions I may find myself, in spite of a fervent desire for the contrary, degenerating into the miserable, well known writer of morbid, or even not morbid, egotistical sentimentality, with few facts and many feelings. But after all, what matters it? My pen will only take my first thoughts as they drift through my mind, without weeding. The writing is for myself. Happily I do not need to make any effort in it.

She did not carry through with her plan to continue the journal. When the couple returned to the United States after their honeymoon, Palmer parked his new wife in Flushing while his dream town took shape. In all honesty he saw it for what it was—a raw, bleak, pioneer town of twelve small, unfinished buildings. It was a far cry from the genteel resort he likened, in his mind, to Newport, Rhode Island. He knew that, in time, Colorado Springs would become the refined town he envisioned, populated by the affluent and well-bred.

While Queen remained in New York, William wrote almost daily to keep her apprised of the growing settlement and to involve her in the building of their Glen Eyrie home:

July 7th, 1871 — Colorado
This is an official letter written purely at the solicitation of Mr.
Whipple who dictates. Do you wish to use inside blind shutters that
fold back into a recess? If you do he must know it immediately as he
must prepare the windows differently. He would recommend them. He
says, don't use outside shutters in this country. 2) What shall be the
colour of priming outside? This he must know immediately; the par-
ticular shade will do after you come out. 3) Please get Dickson's low-
down Philadelphia grates for our fireplaces; they are very handsome.
Mr Whipple is arranging chimney-places for them. 4) The residence
in Glen Eyrie will be scarcely ready for occupancy before the last of
August. Ask your father whether it would not be well for him to go
to government second-hand store-house, Park Place, or elsewhere in
New York to obtain some tents to use until the house is completed. It
would be pleasanter and cheaper than hotel life, even if the hotel were
completed in time, which is doubtful, and would enable your mother
and you to be right on the ground during completion to decide details
of finishing, which is exceedingly important. I suggest one hospital
tent for dining-room, one wall tent and one shelter tent for kitchen and
servants, three wall tents for sleeping. I send you the plan of house
and dimensions by this mail.

Glen Eyrie, July 8th.
It is a cool pleasant morning. What happy days we shall spend here
planning and working to improve our lovely home. Your horse looks
very well and is as kind and gentle as a horse could be.

July 9th, 1871 Glen Eyrie
I am writing to you before arising, in the cabin of our Glen. Last eve-
ning after completing this work I started on Don to go home. It came
on very dark, thundered and lightened and finally the rain fell in

torrents. . . . Don stumbled and came near hurting me severely. I am
not going to let you ride him again. He will make a first-rate carriage
horse with Signor, but I will get you a thoroughly sure-footed well-
trained saddle horse and then we can take our rides together without
any anxiety.

Colorado Springs, July 10th, 1871
You will be glad to learn that I have bought off the land in Camp
Creek Valley for the first mile from the mouth of our Glen southward
towards Colorado City, amounting to 320 acres. It is very rich land
and will raise anything. . . . By the way the Glen, our Glen, has
many wild raspberries in it now. We will have all sorts of fruit there
won't we?

   In order to extirpate the snakes in Glen Eyrie I have directed
James to procure a sow and four pigs and turn them loose. They go
for them like a thousand bricks whenever they see one.

Queen received the happy news from William that her English
friend, Rose Kingsley, would be coming to visit her brother, Maurice
Kingsley, in Colorado, later in the fall. Maurice was secretary of the
Colorado Springs Company, and Rose had made the acquaintance
of the Palmers during their honeymoon in England. She and Queen
became friends.

In camp on the upper Purgatoire, 20 miles above Trinidad, July 18th,
1871;
I was very glad indeed to read Mr. Kingsley's letter and to learn that
Rose was coming over. I wrote at once to Maurice as you requested
and suggested that he should go to St. Louis to meet them.

   I am very sorry that Whipple's plan has been so late in reaching
you. I will write to Mr. Whipple about having the doors for the lower
story all arched and sliding.

The imaginative Queen had the privilege of putting names to the towering spires and unique rock formations in the Glen:

Colorado Springs, July 27th, 1871
You must be thinking of some appropriate names for the different rock shafts and spurs in the glen. General Cameron began suggesting some names yesterday but I stopped him by saying that you were going to name everything in this glen. Mr. Pabor, the poet, has gone up with a guide to Pike's Peak to-day. After his return we shall have printed a very fine description of the ascent and of the scenery enroute. It will come out in the "Tribune" of New York. Be on the look out for it.

General Cameron has just handed me the enclosed for your album, a wild rose plucked from Palmer's Notch. So many people are flocking here that we have deemed it advisable to order the immediate construction of the "Transient Inn," a rough hotel for forty people at the Springs with bath. It will be finished in twenty days.

Major Domo was the name Queen chose for the stately rock that seemed to protect the valley. King Arthur's Seat was a chairlike rock. There was Punchinello, Abraham Lincoln, and Montezuma. A line of spires were fittingly named Echo Rocks. Later, Queen also named the streets of the fledgling town that her Will founded. Some names were French, others Spanish, some were named after rivers and mountains. Cache la Poudre, Huerfano, Conejos, Tejon, Cucharras, Cascade, and Pikes Peak were among them.

Although English settlers in Colorado Springs outnumbered other ethnic groups and nationalities, all were welcome. General Palmer's strong moral code, however, was not optional. William writes to Queen from his camp on the Red River, August 9th, 1871:

I am very glad there is a prospect of a French colony. They will make a graceful and valuable infusion into our more sober pilgrim ele-ment. I wonder how they will get along without wine, however; that

temperance principle is to prevail, you know, among the colonists of
Colorado Springs.

   For our temporary house-keeping in Glen Eyrie you will have to
rely chiefly, I imagine, upon the Denver market. You can have any-
thing sent down on the coach and I hope you will keep yourself sup-
plied plentifully with fruit, for I fear that will be a great deprivation to
you after coming from the fruitful eastern sea-board so recently.

In late October 1871, Queen arrived in Colorado, dressed as a
young bride would for her cavalry hero husband, in a fashionable
Parisian gown. She was accompanied by her father, William Mellen,
stepmother, Ellen, and their six children, Queen's half-brothers,
Nathan, Chase, and Clark, and half-sisters, Helen, Lottie, and Daisy.
General Palmer had invited Mr. Mellen to join him in his railroading
venture.

The group made the journey from New York entirely by train,
since the railroad now extended through the colony. It was an exciting
trip, with herds of buffalo and antelope seen frequently across Kansas.
The ever-changing hues of the grasslands and seemingly endless prairies gave way to the spectacular grandeur of the Rocky Mountains. In
Denver, they changed trains and boarded the General's Denver and
Rio Grande Railroad narrow gauge.

Although thrilled and excited to have finally arrived in the colony,
it must have been disappointing for Queen to be met by Dr. Bell
instead of her William. General Palmer had not yet returned from a
mountain survey. Buckboard wagons took them to Dr. Bell's log cabin
in Manitou.

Will communicated his disappointment in a letter:

I suppose you may now be in Colorado. How I regret not being able
to meet and welcome you back again to the mountains.

Pikes Peak Avenue, 1875–1880, looking west, with snow-
covered Pikes Peak in the background.

(Photo courtesy of Colorado Springs Pioneers Museum)

Colorado Springs, c. 1870. The cottonwood trees thrive
along the nineteen-mile irrigation ditch.

(Photo courtesy of Colorado Springs Pioneers Museum)

A few days later he wrote again:

I think you must be in Colorado by this time, and if so you will get this letter in a very few days. I hope you have not over-exerted yourself in the bustle of moving and that when I reach our tent home in Glen Eyrie I will find you in the best of health.

A tent near a friend's home provided shelter for the newlyweds. Later they lived for a time at the Manitou Hotel, which was simply a shed. Then the stable and hayloft at Glen Eyrie served as their quarters while construction on the house was continuing. Their home would not be ready until mid-winter.

Rose Kingsley arrived in Colorado for a four-month stay. When she returned to England she wrote a colorful book, called *South by West* that was published in 1874. In it she describes her first look at the Pikes Peak area:

> And then began the run down to the Springs, about thirty miles. The road now was picturesque in the extreme, winding along the banks of the Monument Creek, past fantastic sandstone rocks, water-worn into pillars and arches, and great castles with battlemented walls, on the top of every hill. Through the pine trees we now and then caught glimpses of the mountains, pink and purple, towering up ridge over ridge, till, about Husteds [now the Air Force Academy], the whole panorama south of the Divide lay stretched beneath us.
>
> To the right the foothills rose, crowned by the grand snow-covered head of Pike's Peak, 14,336 feet high. To the south, the horizon was bounded by Cheyenne Mountain, standing right out into the plain; and from it to the eastward stretched the boundless prairie.

Rose recorded her impressions of the fledgling town in the middle of nowhere, calling it "Life in a New Town":

> We pulled up at a log cabin by the side of the track, and from the door-way a voice, saying, 'Dinner's on table.' Out we all got, and I thought — surely we can't be going to dine in this place: but M. [Maurice, her brother] took me round to the back door and into the parlour, where he told me to wait while he saw to the luggage. In a few minutes he returned, and took me into the dining room, where I found to my amazement, two large tables on one side, and four small on the other, with clean linen, smart waiters, and a first-rate dinner; far better than any we had had on the Kansas Pacific. I was in a state of complete bewilderment: but hunger soon got the better of surprise, and we were doing ample justice to oyster soup and roast antelope when in came General and Mrs. P. It was pleasant to find well known faces among so many new ones.
>
> You may imagine Colorado Springs, as I did, to be a sequestered valley, with bubbling fountains, green grass, and shady trees; but not a bit of it. Picture to yourself a level elevated plateau of greenish-brown, without a single tree or plant larger than a Spanish bayonet (Yucca) two feet high, sloping down about a quarter of a mile to the railroad track and Monument Creek (the Soda springs being six miles off), and you have a pretty good idea of the town site as it appears in November 1871.
>
> The street and blocks are only marked out by a furrow turned with the plough, and indicated faintly by a wooden house, finished, or in process of building, here and there, scattered over half a mile of prairie. About twelve houses and shanties are inhabited, most of them

being unfinished, or run up for temporary occupation; and there are several tents dotted about also.

On the corner of Tejon and Huerfano Streets stands the office of the Denver and Rio Grande Railway, a small wooden building of three rooms, in which all colony work is done till the new office is finished. It is used, besides, as post-office, doctor's shop, and general lounge for the whole town. My house stands next to it; a wooden shanty, 16 feet by 12, with a door in front, and a small window on each side—they are glass, though they do not open. It is lined with brown paper, so it is perfectly wind-proof, and really quite comfortable, though it was ordered on Thursday and finished on Saturday. M. has now put his tent up over the front of the shanty, with a rough board floor, and it serves for our sitting-room by day and his bedroom at night; so we can warm both the tent and room with a stove in the former. In one corner of the shanty we put my little camp-bed; my trunks in the others. Our furniture had not arrived from Denver; so M. found an old wooden stool, which had been used for mixing paints upon, tacked a bit of coloured calico over it, deposited upon it a tin basin, and there was an impromptu washhand-stand. A few feet of half-inch board were soon converted into corner shelves, and, with warm yellow and red California blankets on my bed, and a buffalo-robe on the floor, my room looked quite habitable. In the tent we have put the stove, a couple of wooden kitchen chairs from the office, and a deal table; M.'s bed makes a comfortable sofa by day; and over the door into the shanty hang two bright curtains Dr. B. [Bell] has brought me from Denver, as a contribution to our housekeeping. In the corner by the stove stands a pail of water; and over it hangs an invaluable tin dipper, which serves for saucepan, glass, jug, cup, and every use imaginable.

A week later Rose tells about a surprise gift that she received to make her temporary home more comfortable, "The P.'s came back from Denver, bringing me a splendid silverback bear robe as a birthday present, which makes our tent look luxurious."

The isolation and loneliness of the raw frontier town was somewhat frightening to any newcomer, and the young Englishwoman, Rose, was no exception:

> I locked myself into my strange new abode, with M.'s revolver as protection against imaginary foes; and by dint of buffalo-robes and blankets, and heaps of flannel, managed to keep tolerably warm, though my breath condensed on the sheets, and when I got up the bucket had a quarter of an inch of ice on it.

The following day the Palmers took Rose to see their dream house in the park, Glen Eyrie. The manor house of Glen Eyrie was being built from lumber brought from the Pinery, which later became known as Black Forest.

Rose Kingsley described her first visit to their home:

Wednesday, Nov. 2 — Drove up to Glen Eyrie with Mrs. P. and General P. and M. followed us up to tea. Glen Eyrie lies about five miles north-west of town, between the Garden of the Gods and Monument park. It is a valley in the foothills, about half a mile long and a little less broad, shut in from the plains by a rock wall, which runs almost from Cheyenne Mountain Park, some fourteen miles, varying in height from fifty feet to some hundred, with here and there a gateway through to some valley or cañon. Into Glen Eyrie debouches one of the finest cañons in the neighbourhood; it has been

*explored for ten miles into the mountains, and goes on no one knows
how much farther. At the very mouth of the cañon, close to a beautiful group of Douglassii pine, and just above the little rushing mountain torrent, which used to be known to trappers as "Camp Creek,"
the P.'s are building a most charming large house, but till it is finished
they live in a sort of picnic way, in rooms 10 x 10, partitioned off
from the loft over the stable. There was just room for us all four to sit
at tea and we had great fun. There were four cups, but no saucers,
and we had borrowed two forks from the restaurant, so that we each
had one. Their coloured servant had cooked some excellent venison
and flapjacks for us, and we had Californian honey, blackberry pre-
serve, first-rate coffee and baked potatoes.*

Queen Palmer was herself well educated and even at age twenty-
one she realized the importance of education. She took it upon herself
to open the first school for the children of the colony. She rented a
three-room house on Cascade Avenue until a proper school could be
built. On opening day she had seven enthusiastic pupils and in a very
short time that number had grown to twenty.

William wrote to Queen from Cañon City, Colorado, on September
30th, 1871, encouraging her involvement in the schooling of the colony's children. His pride in her endeavor was obvious:

*Is the school-house coming along to your satisfaction and have the
roads been begun yet? I can scarcely tell you how glad I am to see
you so much interested in the school. You will succeed admirably, for
I have never met anyone better fitted to manage and win and instruct
little ones, your heart being so thoroughly in the work that I am
sure you will see that none of those who are to be the future men and
women of our pet town shall grow up ignorant or bad, if you can
help it.*

The *Rocky Mountain News*, published on November 18, 1871, announced the opening of the school:

> A public school is in operation at the new town, and is taught by Mrs. General Palmer. We saw quite a number of rosy-cheeked, light-haired little misses tripping gaily to school in the early morning, and several young lads were availing themselves of the same glorious privileges. The motive that prompted a wealthy, refined, and educated lady to inaugurate and personally superintend this primitive educational institution is, to say the least, a worthy example, and such an act of christian charity as we deem highly commendable.

In *South by West* Rose Kingsley tells about a school incident that demonstrated to her the surprising equality of the American people:

> The school is flourishing and every one is pleased. I went up to see it yesterday. It was just recess-time, and the children were getting their luncheon. A daughter of M.'s washerwoman came, and said "Good-morning" to me, with a kiss, which I did not receive with due gratitude, as she had evidently breakfasted off garlic. But this is a free country, where the washerwoman is as good as I; and consequently I must submit, with smiling submission, to being kissed by her daughter.

Several weeks later, Rose had the opportunity to try her own hand at teaching:

> *I have been teaching school for two days!*
>
> *I got a telegram last Monday from the P's [Palmers], who are in Denver, to say they were detained; so I went up to the school,*

intending to send the children home. But when I got there I found more than twenty children assembled outside in the snow, and they were so anxious to have school that at last I consented to stop and teach them myself. The door was locked: so I made two of the bigger boys get in through a window, and following them in unfastened the door, and we soon lit the stove and set to work. They were of all ages, from five to fifteen, so that it was rather a difficult matter to keep them all at work at once.

The school was later moved from the rented house, which belonged to the town's publicist and secretary, Mr. Pabor, to the second floor of the newspaper office on the northeast corner of Tejon and Colorado. Mrs. Liller, the editor's wife, took over as teacher, with her salary being paid by the Palmers.

The Second Biennial Report of the Superintendent of Public Instruction of the Territory of Colorado, for the two years ending September 30, 1873, states, "The foundation of a fine school building has been laid at Colorado Springs, in which, when it is completed, we hope to have a first-class graded school."

A harsh blizzard ushered in the winter of 1871, causing the broad-gauge trains from Kansas City to reach Denver three days late. Rose Kingsley explains that the narrow gauge trains fared better:

The snow was drifting tremendously, the strong wind lifting the dry powdery particles off the ground, and blowing it across the plain in clouds of white dust. The thermometer outside the house registered 13° above zero. . . . The train, we thought, would of course be stopped by drifts on the divide: but it was only one hour late; and, in the middle of dinner, in it steamed. It was really a fine sight. The little 'Cortez' had been through the snow-drifts, up to the top of the lamp in front of the chimney. The wheels, and every ledge and corner, were a mass of snow, and the icicles hung in a crystal fringe all along the boiler.

The snow continued to plague the railroads and the cold made life miserable. Rose continues:

> They joined company, every man turning out and digging in the snow for four hours; by which means, and by driving the engine against the snow full speed, they got through at last.
>
> This fall of snow is exceptionally heavy . . . with the high wind we have had it drift badly, and packs into a much closer mass than our usual Western snow.
>
> The narrow gauge still holds its own against the broad gauge, and a freight train got through behind the passengercars yesterday; while on the Union and Kansas Pacific Railroads no freight has got through for two weeks, and all the passenger trains have come into Denver one to four days late. There have been two feet of snow for the last week in Denver, and every one is sleighing who can afford it; while the sleigh-owners are making small fortunes by charging eight to ten dollars an hour.

The delay of the freight trains caused great concern among the settlers needing supplies. Hunting wild game became a necessity to supplement their dwindling staples, though not always successfully. In *South by West* Rose writes:

> The "cold snap" has driven large herds of antelopes in from the plains to the shelter of the bluffs, and yesterday, hearing there were some near town, M. [Maurice] and I had out the ambulance with the mules, and drove off in

search of them, armed with a revolver. We had not gone more than a mile and a half west of the town site when we saw a herd in a hollow to the right of the road. M. got out and crept away after the antelope, telling me to drive slowly after him. There were about twenty-three, and when we had crossed the hollow and got to the top of the next rise, we saw an immense herd of some hundreds a mile west. I watched M. along the crest of the hill, the antelope meanwhile running round below him out of sight, when suddenly he stopped. Piff, piff, piff went the pistol and I drove on to him. No luck, alas! As Butler, the negro at the office, had loaded the revolver, and carefully put in half charges; so every shot fell short.

The antelopes are so starved this winter that they are coming in by thousands off the plains all along the base of the mountains. At Greeley, the colony town north of Denver, they come among the houses and get shot from the windows. A herd of forty was crowded in a field, and the Greeleyites went out and surrounding it shot them all down, poor little things! They are so pretty, it seems cruel to kill them in this unsportsmanlike manner.

Frances M. Wolcott, in *Heritage of Years*, reported also that the winter was unusually harsh. "The oldest inhabitant never knew such thirty consecutive days of cold, often ten degrees below zero."

November 28, was an important date in the life of the new community. Rose Kinsgley explains:

Yesterday was bright but horribly cold. The trees by the creek had each twig covered with rime half an inch thick, from a dense fog which had frozen upon them the night before. It was an important day to us; as the Fountain Ditch, i.e. the irrigating ditch by which the water from the Fountain above Colorado Springs, is to be brought down to irrigate the town site at Colorado Springs, was finished.

Yesterday the water was turned in, and so we hoped that it was slowly making its way down the ditch last night towards us; though, as the ditch is 11 1/2 miles long, having to be carried round hill-sides and over gullies, it will take some time to fill it thoroughly.

On Thanksgiving Day, November, 30, fickle Mother Nature smiled on Colorado Springs:

The snow is gone, and the sun blazing in a cloudless sky. I watched avalanches falling on Pike's Peak all the morning, and after each the cloud of snow-smoke rising, and blowing round the top of the mountain. Today is such a contrast to the last three days, which have been so bitter we have only left the house for our meals, and then rushed down muffled up in every wrap we possessed to keep out the wind.

Garden of the Gods was waiting to be explored and Rose Kingsley found it incredibly beautiful:

Drove along what was dignified by the name of a road; though it more resembled a newly-dug celery trenches, varied by gravel-pits, and a deep ditch right across every few hundred feet. At last we got into the Outer Garden, a great open space of grass under the foothills, with scattered pines, and here and there fantastic sandstone rocks; and further on, to our right, lay the great rocks, the real wonder of the Garden. We passed many weird-like figures praying, with their heads all bent towards Cheyenne Mountains; then a red sandstone nun, with white cowl over her head, looking at a seal who stood on his tail and made faces at her. There, I was told, two cherubs were fondly kissing, though to my eyes I confess they looked more like a pair of sheep's heads [the famous Kissing Camels]; and so find new absurdities every moment, we came to the great gateway; drove between the huge red rocks, 250 feet high; and turned to see the view. It surpasses everything I have yet seen.

The great rocks were of a warm salmon colour, with green pines growing in their crevices, bringing out the richness of their colouring and between them, as if set in a glowing frame, shone Pike's Peak, covered in snow, as a centre to the picture, with Cameron's Cone and the foot-hills, all blue, white, and pink, three or four miles off.

I wish everyone at home could see this view. No descriptions or photographs can do it justice; and as for drawing it—who can do that?

The early snows of November certainly delayed construction of Glen Eyrie, but it was progressing. Queen and Rose took advantage of the break in the weather for an excursion:

Mrs. P. asked me to drive up to Glen Eyrie with her, and explore the Camp Creek Cañon, above the house. Anything more lovely I never saw. At the entrance of the cañon the coloured rock-walls are about a stone's-throw apart; and the ravine on either side of the clear foaming stream is filled with a rich growth of trees and shrubs, festooned with Virginia creeper and wild clematis. Further up the walls close in; and we scrambled up, crossing and recrossing the stream every few yards, by fallen timber and boulders under lofty pines and cottonwoods, till we came to the "Punch Bowl." The stream has scooped itself out a round path in the red and white streaked rocks, which rise high above the bed of the stream. The basin is about twenty feet across, and fills up the whole cañon. The water falls into it over steps of rock; and above it the cañon winds up into the mountains, no one knows how far, as only a few miles of it have been as yet explored. About two miles up are some beautiful falls, which M. [Maurice] discovered last year: but as the only way across the Punch Bowl was by a single log of pine, very thin and covered with ice, and as I was wet through from wading through the snow, which was quite deep in some places, I did not feel inclined to risk the chance of an icy bath, but determined to see the falls some other time, and we turned back to Glen Eyrie for dinner and dry shoes.

General P. and Professor H. of Madison, Wisconsin, came up, and we started, as the sun set and the moon rose, to explore the upper end of Glen Eyrie. The moon looked so tempting over the crest of the hill that we set off on a track that leads up the high ridge dividing Glen Eyrie from the Upper Garden. After we had passed the great Echo Rocks, and made them sing two or three songs a couple of bars behind us, a narrow track led us to the top with a scramble; and once there, the view was really superb. To the right, on the crest of the hill, was a group of pines, through which the moon shone so brightly, it was like white daylight. Behind us lay the Glen, with its strange red rocks, and the hills rising up to old Pike all covered with snow; and in front of us another deep valley, shut in with another wall of rock, widening out into a park above, and below narrowing into a cañon which apparently had no exit. None of us had ever been there before: but we plunged down the hill through deep snow, with here and there a Spanish bayonet sticking up to prick the unwary, down to the bed of the cañon. It was so narrow that only one person at a time could squeeze along between the rocks; and I began seriously to fear it would soon get too narrow for us to escape, and that we should have to stay there for the rest of our days. Suddenly, however, out of the intense black shade, we came into a streak of brilliant moonlight, which streamed through a cleft in the rocks before us not more than three feet wide; and we saw we were at the gate of the cañon with the outer valley in dazzling light beyond.

We sat still for a few minutes to gaze in delight through the rock; then squeezed between them with some little difficulty, and looking back, could not see the passage by which we had emerged. It seemed as if we had broken through the lower panes of a Gothic window, which had been partly filled up with stone.

Turning to the right we went up a high snow-covered hill to the foot of the outer wall of the Garden, more than 7000 feet above the sea. This wall is a mass of rock from fifty to three hundred feet high, and in some places not more than eighteen feet thick, running along the top line of hills made apparently of debris of old rocks, and extending from near Cheyenne Mountain to Monument Park, with here and there an opening into one or other of the gardens or parks, where some creek has sawn its way through.

It was a stiff climb through the snow, in the intensely rarefied air, which completely takes one's breath away going up hill; and for five minutes after we reached the top I felt as if my chest had been scraped raw; but after a little while this sensation went off. Going down was much pleasanter than getting up, and in a little while we were wading through the snow and mud up to the stable, where the P.'s are still living, as their house is not finished. After supper and a very pleasant evening, Professor H. drove me home, and we found M. waiting to receive us.

Christmas was a gay celebration for the hardy settlers. The town had its first Christmas tree and twenty couples attended a gala ball at Foote's Hall. Queen hosted a Christmas party for the children, setting a precedent that continued for many years.

An historic event heralded the beginning of the New Year of 1872.

Colorado Springs Hotel, opened New Year's Day, 1872,
the pride of the pioneer town.
(Photo courtesy Pikes Peak Library District, Local History Collection)

The Colorado Springs Hotel opened on January 1st. It was a momentous occasion for the town, as Rose Kingsley attested:

> January 1, 1872 — The new year has come in with bright sun, no wind, and cloudless blue sky. It is a marked day in the life of our little colony; for after two months of delays the Colorado Springs Hotel was opened at 2 P.M., and we went to our first meal there, and ate with English knives and forks, off English china, a first rate dinner.

The southeast corner of Cascade and Colorado Avenue, c. 1874. The Colorado Springs Hotel is at the far left.

(Photo courtesy of Colorado Springs Pioneers Museum)

New Year's Day also brought an unexpected visit from a party of Utes from New Mexico. The townspeople were relieved to see that squaws accompanied the party, assuring the populace that it was a peaceful group: One of the braves is described in *South by West*:

> He had on a scarlet blanket over buckskins, a kind of breastplate of beads, mostly white; and a row of silver beads down the parting of his hair, ending on his forehead with a silver crescent. . . . Some of their faces were painted with red stripes; and one had red and yellow stripes on the cheeks, yellow being the second mourning for a near relation. . . . The Ute war-paint . . . is black and white.

The Indians were fascinated by the railroad, "the first they had ever seen and squatted down, rubbing the metals with their fingers." Some even ventured to take their first ride to Denver on this unusual contraption. The group set up camp near Manitou for a leisurely stay and to hunt in the mountains.

With great anticipation the first service was held by the Episcopal Church in Foote's Hall. Rose writes:

> Saturday, January 12—As M. was away at Pueblo, Mrs. P. brought me up to Manitou yesterday; and this morning we have been roaming up the cañons, collecting seeds and stones. A white spirea grows here in great quantities, and when it is in flower I am told it looks like powdered snow among the green leaves. The day was so hot that we could not bear jackets over our gowns. After luncheon we walked down to the beaver dam, on the Fountain, and got some chips from the trees the beavers have felled. They are exactly the shape of ordinary chips cut with a hatchet, from an inch to three inches across.

To-morrow we are going to have our first Episcopal service in the town; Mr. E., the clergyman from Pueblo, having offered to come for a Sunday; and we hope that till a church is built here, the Bishop will be able to send us a clergyman once a month. We are determined to begin with as good a service as possible; we have had several practices this week for it, and had our final one this afternoon. Mr. E. arrived on the coach; and I found that he was not only an Englishman, but came from Marlowe, so we had a pleasant talk over all our Berkshire friends.

Sunday, 13th—A lovely day. A little before 11 A.M. we went over to Foote's Hall, where the service was to be held. I had Mrs. P.'s harmonium over from the school, and we managed the Canticles and two hymns very creditably, most of the congregation joining in. There were sixty-five people present, a good many of whom were Methodists, etc., but the larger proportion Episcopalians. As no one else seemed inclined to lead the responses, I did.

In late January of 1872 a concert was held to help raise funds for a Reading Room and Library, a necessary addition to the culture-starved colony.

Queen's mezzo-soprano voice was delightful entertainment at the local fundraiser, and Rose Kingsley was the accompanist. As she described, it was a welcome diversion from the difficulties of frontier life:

Temporary Inn, Manitou, Jan. 19—I came up here a week ago to pay a visit to General and Mrs. P., who are living here till Glen Eyrie is finished, and we are very busy preparing for a concert. The reading-room is in want of funds, so we have determined to give a concert for its benefit; and have enlisted all the musical talent of the neighbourhood to help us.

Jan. 28, Manitou—Our concert is over, and has been a great success, in spite of the cold. After a month of perfect weather we have had a "cold snap," and the thermometer was down to 22° below zero.

On the 24th there was a dense snowy fog, and the thermometer never rose above zero all day, and when we met in the evening at the L.'s for a practice, it was 19° below. We were nearly frozen. We put the piano close to the stove and between each verse of the songs which I was accompanying, I had to jump up and put my fingers into the open stove door to thaw them; for they were quite numb from touching the keys.

On Thursday, the day of the concert, the weather was a little less severe. Practices of one kind or other were going on from early morning and we had a full rehearsal in the afternoon as soon as the southern stage came in; for it brought a bass viol and its owner from fifteen miles down the Fountain. He made a most imposing foundation to the "concerted pieces."

We colonists hitherto have not been able to indulge much in evening dress, though doubtless that will come soon with our rapidly growing civilisation; and a thick tweed gown has served me for morning and evening, Sunday and week-day alike, ever since I came here three months ago.

The concert was advertised for 7:30, but we did not all get together till nearly eight; and by that time Foote's Hall, which at present is used for every sort of public gathering, was crowded with an orderly audience of about 150, of all classes, down to "bull-whackers" who dropped in after their day's work with the ox and mule teams.

At last all was ready. Captain de C. appeared with a jug of egg-nogg [sic] under his coat, which was cunningly deposited under the piano, so that as the performers went up to the very shaky platform they could stoop down and refresh themselves unseen; and the concert opened with a chorus. Everything went well. The bass viol, who I found had only tried his instrument a fortnight before, scraped away and tuned his strings, which insisted on getting out of tune every six bars. Our prima donna Mrs. P., and M., got rapturous applause. Mrs. P. sang a scena of Verdi's and two or three popular ballads; and M. began with "The fox went out on a Moonlight

Glen Eyrie, nestled in the wooded valley, was at long last ready for the Palmer family in February, 1872.

(Photo courtesy of Colorado Springs Pioneers Museum)

Night." Which was so successful that he had to sing two other songs as encores.

All went home delighted with their evening. The result to the reading-room was most satisfactory, as after all expenses were paid we netted $60 (£12 sterling), a creditable amount for a town only five months old.

In February the Palmers happily moved into their new home. Glen Eyrie would undergo further additions and renovations in 1881–1882.

Queen's friend, Rose Kingsley, moved to Glen Eyrie with them to help them get settled—not an easy matter, as she observed:

> I am sitting writing in the cañon, under a grove of cotton-wood, Douglassii fir, and silver spruce. My chair is a lump of red granite, with a wall of the same rising behind me reflecting the hot sun, so that I begin to feel like your idea of perfect bliss—a lizard on a hot white wall. The creek frozen solid, gleams white, at my feet; and opposite rises the south wall of the cañon, 800 to 1000 feet high; red, pink, and salmon rocks show through the pine and pinons, which cover them; and all is in black shade, save the streaks of snow which lies here and there still unmelted.
>
> There is not a sound except the sighing of a breeze in the pines, or the scream of a blue jay as he flashes past in the sunlight, and scolds at finding me intruding on his solitude; or when a solitary half-tame sheep that haunts this valley comes rustling down through the scrub-oak off the mountains to drink at the creek. The air is full of the scent from the cotton-wood, which is beginning to bud; and a fly settles on my paper to rest after his first flight in the spring sunshine.

We moved over here to Glen Eyrie, General P.'s lovely house, which has been building for the last six months, and is at last finished enough for us to get into it, though it is still haunted by armies of painters, etc. It is built close to the mouth of the cañon I am writing in, on the slope of the hill, with the glen stretched out before it dotted with tall pines and fantastic rocks of every colour except bright blue, shutting it in from the outer world.

I have been very busy since we came, helping my kind hostess to settle in—no easy matter in this servantless land—where one has to do most things for one's-self. The want of servants in the West is a very serious difficulty, and one it seems almost impossible to overcome.

Pikes Peak Avenue, c. 1883, with utility poles lining the streets of the village dubbed "Little London."

(Photo courtesy of Colorado Springs Pioneers Museum)

They are simply not to be had, whatever you pay them. One of our neighbours has been trying the whole of this winter to get a servant, sending to Denver, Georgetown, Central. . . . After doing all her own house-work, and cooking for her own family and several boarders for two months, she got a girl at last from a ranche [sic] in the mountains, who thought she would like a change. To this creature, who could not cook or make herself useful in any way, except in actual scrubbing, she paid $25 (£5) a month, board, lodging . . . and before the month was out the young lady found Colorado Springs was 'too dull for her,' and went off to Denver, leaving my friend servantless again.

As I am writing this, I heard voices coming up the cañon; and soon Mrs. P. appeared, bringing several of our Denver friends who are down at the hotel. We all scrambled up the cañon, along the ice-covered stream, with birds singing among the pine tops in the sunshine overhead. We made our way above the Punch Bowl, which is now, with the waterfall, a mass of solid ice, to Daphne's Leap, a beautiful bubbling spring under a group of pines; and as we stood there, a noble eagle flew over our heads, so close that we could see his yellow gleaming eye looking down on us as we held our breath in surprise and delight.

By springtime Colorado Springs could boast of a population of seven or eight hundred. A nineteen mile irrigation ditch brought water to an additional thirteen miles of smaller ditches and six hundred young cottonwood trees were brought from Arkansas to be planted along the dusty streets of the fledgling town. Gardens added to the green freshness of spring and fresh fruits and vegetables were anticipated with great enthusiasm.

The settlers had been carefully chosen, as General Palmer had intended, but not everyone saw the potential that General Palmer envisioned. Rose Kingsley tells of her brother's effort to comfort a newly arrived English family who were shocked and disillusioned to see what the pioneer town actually looked like:

> February 26th—In the afternoon, while I was waiting for M. in the office, some colonists—a man, his wife, and three children—came in, having come down by the train. They were English, from Southampton, and utterly disgusted and disheartened, of course, by the place at first sight. They expected a large town, with fine farming lands, ready ploughed and fenced, all round. They had no bedding, nor any necessaries for life in a shanty. The baby was ill, the little girl crying with fatigue and bewilderment, the father cross, and the mother dirty. M. put them for the night into our old shanty, which happened to be vacant, and gave them his own bed, as they were from the old country, though they were disagreeable enough, goodness knows.
>
> But never will I persuade people to emigrate after seeing these and other colonists, utterly unprepared for the sort of life they will have to lead. Thinking that a town here means what it does in England; that farming lands—which, in truth, are good enough when they are irrigated and properly farmed—are to be like a rich bit of Hertfordshire or the Vale of Thames; and finding what it is in reality, they turn round and accuse those who have advised them to leave the struggle for existence in the old country, of sending them to their death and ruin in the new.

There were reports of two incensed immigrants who threatened to shoot the authors of the pamphlet that had encouraged their defection from their previous homes. They fumed about the primitive conditions and referred to the farm land as "nothing but a gravel patch."

In a short time, however, most of the disgruntled newcomers were won over. The wild beauty of the mountain backdrop, the ever changing colors of the plains, the pure, exhilarating air, the sparkling waters of the natural springs, and the incredible spirit of the townspeople soon transformed them into dedicated pioneers. Indeed it was not the Utopia that General Palmer envisioned, but it was a beginning! It was soon dubbed "Little London."

In early March, Queen accompanied William on an arduous trip to Mexico City. The General hoped to smooth the way toward extending his narrow gauge rails into Mexico. They were joined by Rose Kingsley.

The proposed trip to a foreign land and culture was exciting. They studied the Spanish language and read everything they could find about Mexico in anticipation of the adventure to the "land of enchantment." It also heralded an end to Rose Kingsley's visit to America. She writes:

> March 4 — To-morrow we start. All our preparations are made; M. and the five others of the engineering party leave by the overland stage; and the P.'s and I go north on our way to San Francisco. . . . It is sad to leave so many dear and kind friends whom I seem to have known for years instead of months: not knowing whether most of us may ever meet again.
>
> If anything had been needed to make me believe in the kindness, generosity, and warm-hearted friendship of Americans, the four months I have spent here would have proved to me — what I knew already — that in no country on earth can one find better and truer friends than in the United States.

The group traveled by stagecoach to California. From there they boarded a steamer, *Alaska*, to take them to the Mexican port of Manzanillo.

Mexico was in a state of unrest, having recently put down a revolution. Crossing the Gulf of California provided the time for General Palmer to teach the women how to handle a gun.

With the men on horseback and mules hauling the huge trunks, the women climbed aboard an old carriage to complete the journey. It was a harrowing trip. Near the outskirts of a large town, they were attacked by a band of highwaymen but escaped without injury.

The endless hours of uncomfortable travel, the primitive accommodations along the way, the fear spawned during the nights spent in unsecured hotels and haciendas took their toll on the exhausted Colorado party. Queen was not well. Perhaps it was later that the reason became obvious to everyone. Slightly less than eight months after starting the tortuous journey, their first daughter, Elsie, was born.

Close to the end of their travel they were joined by an overland party of engineers who had left Colorado about the same time. That party included General Hunt, the former territorial governor of Colorado.

It must have been a great relief for the entire party when, on April 26, 1872, they rode into Mexico City. They had been traveling for over a month.

The Colorado party stayed at the Hotel Iturbide. In the relative safety and comfort of Mexican hospitality, Queen felt better.

Palmer met with anyone influential enough to help in his cause of extending the railroad. He discussed his plans with politicians and government ministers hoping to persuade them to support his plans. William wrote to his father-in-law on May 24th telling him that the prospects of seeing his dream become reality looked promising. The general then joined the group of engineers to explore the possible train route.

The ladies stayed in Mexico City, enjoying the sights. They visited Chapultepec, overlooking the city, which once was the site of an ancient temple honoring the Aztec rain god, Tlaloc. In 1780 construction was started on a palace for viceroys at the same location. The most famous occupants of the Castle were the ill-fated romantic couple, Maximilian and Carlota. Maximilian ruled as emperor of Mexico from 1864 to 1867. During that time, the French, who had supported his reign, withdrew, but the emperor stayed, believing he had the support of the Mexican people. He was executed by firing squad after being captured by the Mexican Republican forces. Queen's visit occurred barely four years later. The German priest who had been Maximilian's confessor was the tour guide for the ladies.

As soon as William returned to Mexico City from his exploration of the countryside with the engineers from Colorado, the Palmer party headed for home. The return trip took them over the mountains by coach and part way by rail. From Vera Cruz they sailed to Havana, Cuba, and to Cedar Key on the west coast of Florida. From there the train took them through the south to Richmond, Virginia, and on to New York where Queen stayed for the birth of their daughter. Elsie was born on October 30, 1872.

A reproduction of a picture of Queen in authentic Mexican dress was published years later in the Fifty-First Annual Edition of the Colorado Springs *Gazette Telegraph* (April 8, 1923). It shows a charming Queen, curly tendrils of dark hair escaping from her upswept hairstyle, during one of the happiest, most triumphant times of her life. The diplomatic team of William and Queen was a success.

General Palmer again traveled to Mexico in December 1872, hoping to solidify his position with the Mexican government. Unfortunately the contracts and negotiations that the general and his agents had worked so hard to achieve collapsed and were revived only briefly several years later.

Back home in Colorado the young family grew and prospered. The new city was growing fast. William, involved not only in the rail line but also in the coal and iron fields of southern Colorado, traveled a great deal.

Queen's family, the Mellens, traveled to Colorado, where they remained. Queen's stepmother, Ellen, had a baby named Maud who was born about the same time that Queen's little Elsie was born. Watching their babies grow gave the two women much to share.

For many years a band of Ute Indians, headed by Chief Washington, had camped out in the glen near the stream. The Indians were very curious about the white family's way of life, sometimes wandering uninvited throughout the house or peering through the glass windows.

The chief invited the family to a feast at the Indian camp, and with some trepidation Queen and Ellen accepted, for the general and Mellen were away on business. The ladies and the children presented trinkets and jewelry as gifts to the Indians and were welcomed wholeheartedly.

Rhoda Wilcox, in her book *Man on the Iron Horse*, tells the story of a young brave, named Happy Jack, and his squaw, who appeared at the door of the Glen Eyrie nursery where Queen and Ellen were bathing their babies. The pretty Indian mother had brought her papoose with her. In English learned at a mission school she asked the women to bathe her baby. They unwrapped the strips of cloth that held the baby to its board, bathed and powdered her. They dressed her in white baby clothes as the proud mother watched, dark eyes shining. She called her husband to admire the baby, and as the young family left, the Indian woman promised, "I remember you all the days of my life."

That same year William Proctor Mellen, Queen's father, died. General Palmer, as he had promised, became surrogate father to the Mellen children that he had come to love as his own.

Spirited as ever, Queen continued her numerous forays into Queen's Canyon. As author Frances M. Wolcott said:

> Finding unknown heights and following streams to their sources, was to make excursions of rare delight.

Queen Palmer, climbing stock in hand, rebellious curly hair flying, cheeks aglow, moving as on winged feet, was the spirit incarnate of inaccessible heights. Hats she scorned. She laid claim to beauty as her rightful heritage, whether in a moated English house in Surrey or in the spacious room in the third story of "Glen Eyrie" where she gathered books, heard musicians and never permitted any but an invited friend to enter.

Indeed, Queen remained unsubdued, in spite of the numerous rattlesnakes that inhabited the rocky cliffs of Glen Eyrie. Mountain lion and bobcat, too, wandered through the estate as they always had. Bighorn sheep and deer munched on the tender blades of grass and drank from the tumbling waters of the crystal clear creek. Black bear, some cinnamon colored, others truly black, lumbered through the forest but could quickly and effortlessly scale the steep rocks. Falcons and eagles perched on the highest pinnacles. Flickers and jays, some brilliant blue and others dove gray, settled in the branches of the blue spruce and pine trees. Tiny hummingbirds flitted among the aspen.

In the dark of night the howl of coyotes could be heard, echoing across the glen, and owls silently swooped over the tall trees or hooted softly from a high branch. Porcupine and raccoon rustled through the dense scrub oak.

Wildflowers carpeted the slopes. One of the earliest to herald spring was the creamy sego lily, and soon the soft blue of the columbine contrasted with the bright red paintbrush. Wild strawberry struggled through unseen clefts in the rocks and in late summer the sweet raspberries hung heavy on the bushes.

Queen excelled as hostess to Palmer's friends and business associates, exuding warmth and unfailing kindness. F. C. Thornton, who later would write of Queen's life in a Colorado Springs *Gazette Telegraph* article printed in 1923, was a visitor at Glen Eyrie in 1872. He was a stranger to the Palmers, and had been brought there by a mutual friend his first day in Colorado. Queen quickly put him at ease, and he found her absolutely charming and unpretentious.

The importance of Glen Eyrie increased as General Palmer's undertakings developed. Many influential men and women were entertained there. Queen had indeed become the ideal hostess that William had envisioned. He delighted in her ability.

Queen Palmer
(Photo courtesy of Colorado Springs Pioneers Museum)

Glen Eyrie underwent renovation in 1881 and 1882. The rock
formation in the background is Major Domo.

(Photo courtesy of Colorado Springs Pioneers Museum)

Queen Palmer on the rock wall spanning the creek at Glen
Eyrie. The photo has been damaged.

(Photo courtesy of Colorado Springs Pioneers Museum)

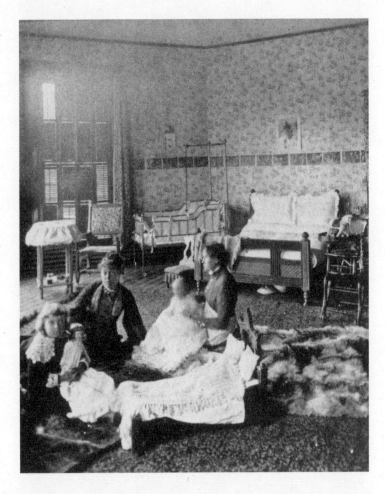

Queen with eight-year-old Elsie and Tante, holding Dorothy,
in the nursery at Glen Eyrie, 1880.

(Photo courtesy of Colorado Springs Pioneers Museum)

Tante, the children's nanny, holding one-year-old Dorothy.

(Photo courtesy of Colorado Springs Pioneers Museum)

Marjory Palmer at seven months old. She was born in England
on November 12, 1881.

(Photo courtesy of Colorado Springs Pioneers Museum)

Dorothy Palmer, two and a half years old, May 12, 1883. She was the only one of the Palmers' daughters born in Colorado.

(Photo courtesy of Colorado Springs Pioneers Museum)

Mrs. Wolcott, author, describes a hazardous mountain ride with the Palmers when the weather changed suddenly, dropping forty degrees in as many minutes. A dust storm and an icy gale blew in from the north, making it difficult to even see each other. "We must trust to the wisdom of the horses to find their way" was Palmer's calm advice, and, almost frozen, blinded by the dust, and with faces caked with dirt, they safely returned home to a cozy fire and hot dinner.

For a time the Palmers suffered a reversal of fortune when it became necessary for William to put most of his assets behind his railroad expansion. They could not afford to keep Glen Eyrie open and moved temporarily into a cottage on Cascade Avenue. Mr. Thornton visited there with his wife, and they found that Queen remained the same moving spirit of Colorado Springs. In her subdued surroundings, she was still the generous hostess who had graced the manor house. Her behavior during that time exhibited her loyalty to William and her strength of purpose as he threw his entire personal fortune behind his pioneering endeavors.

In the summer of 1880, Queen and her English friend, Alma Strettell, took a sightseeing trip to Leadville. Miss Strettell came to Colorado to be with her brother, who was not in good health. She and Queen became friends. It was an exciting drive to the wild little town that nestled among the mountains at an altitude above ten thousand feet. Queen's guest was surprised to see that there was a pistol in the picnic basket her hostess had brought. It was on their return trip that the first of Queen's heart attacks occurred.

It was a frightening episode, but Queen was only thirty years old and it is possible that no one recognized the seriousness of her condition. It probably didn't occur to her or her family that the episode was a forewarning of health problems that would forever alter the course of her life.

Later that year, on October 29, 1880, their second daughter, Dorothy, was born in Colorado.

The next year the family went to England, where Marjory was

Glen Eyrie with its outbuildings visible behind the house.
(Photo courtesy Colorado Springs Pioneers Museum)

Glen Eyrie, front view. Two hammocks hang
in the observation tower addition.
(Photo courtesy of Colorado Springs Pioneers Museum)

Queen Palmer at Glen Eyrie

(Photo courtesy of Colorado Springs Pioneers Museum)

The gatehouse at the entry of the Glen Eyrie property.

(Photo courtesy Colorado Springs Pioneers Museum)

born on November 12, 1881. In early 1882 General Palmer returned from Europe to make yet another trip to Mexico, leaving his family in the charming seaside resort town of Eastbourne, in southeastern England, which was on the English Channel and was known for its mild, sunny climate.

Though not with his family, William wanted to be closely involved with his daughters' upbringing. He wrote to Queen from the *Whitney*, somewhere in the Gulf of Mexico on April 26th, 1882:

The sea is smooth and the sky serene and if we had any cargo the ship would be very steady.

Your remark about Elsie being dull-eyed and wan, under so healthful a location as London and using so much of the best sort of exercise as she does, raises an important question. You speak of her busy day and how exactly the hours are apportioned off. It sounds like a great deal for so little a body. The strain on so tender a mind and attention may be too wearing. Is the discipline too much and are the rules too exacting for a rather delicate constitution? At her age her father was taxed too much in that same way. It was terminated in his case by a long illness, which came near being fatal. . . . I suppose the nearer to little kittens children can actually be kept during infancy the better, so as to give the animal part of their natures full swing and development. The brain will do all the better through all the future life for this stout basis and support, instead of as otherwise, finding mental operations like a dull knife, always afterwards a tax and labour and drag. A child is, however, learning all the same, but is taking in quietly and slowly those simple impressions which really mold the character permanently. Languages and everything else are insignificant compared with this: a quiet, clean, unexcited, orderly nurse, of as much practical good sense as possible, very matter of fact and lazily good natured, an utter absence of morbidness; one who would make the nursery a cheerful comfortable room, tell them the good old nursery rhymes in simple fashion, teach them needlework and the old-fashioned ideas so conducive to contentment and ease and usefulness. There may be too much of a hot-house tendency nowadays in our ideas about children, as if the competitions of the business and social world had entered the nursery and the schoolhouse, and too little of the slow healthy growth which permits the best developments through all the stages of the body and mind. We are so ambitious for her that we may have driven her too much, in our anxious zeal, and made a little machine of her.

Dorothy, Elsie, Marjory, and other children at the schoolhouse built near the Glen Eyrie home. Palmer feared the possibility of kidnapping by rival railroads as they fought over rights through the Royal Gorge.

(Photo courtesy of Colorado Springs Pioneers Museum)

Later he responded to news of his oldest daughter's ability as a horsewoman:

I am perfectly enchanted to learn of the way Elsie jumps. She has succeeded beyond even my sanguine hopes. Little Dorothy, I suppose will soon be wanting to jump also.

In May General Palmer returned to England, bringing his mother with him. The elder Mrs. Palmer had moved from Philadelphia to St. Louis, and from St. Louis to Colorado, to be near her son. Her granddaughter, Elsie, in later years was to describe her grandmother as a very gentle, serene little Quaker lady. After a stay of several months, the entire family returned to Glen Eyrie.

The general's varied business endeavors took him away from Glen Eyrie frequently, sometimes for long periods of time. He stayed in touch with his family by mail. While on one such trip he wrote a somewhat whimsical letter to eleven-year-old Elsie. He used the opportunity to discuss a natural phenomenon that was of interest to both of them. From Buckingham Hotel at Fifth Avenue and 50th St. in New York, William wrote to his daughter:

Sunday, Dec. 30, 1883
My Darling little Elsie,
I did not I believe answer your letter of the 21st. Your way of finding out what the servants would like for Xmas was a very good one. You thereby avoided the risk of giving presents that would not be of real use or be truly wanted & appreciated by them.

If poor Gilloo [sic] but only knew, the way we do — when I and you — our brains do stew — with verses few — some old some new — both false and true.

I do believe
He ne'er would leave
His Denver home

Again to roam
So far and wide
South of the Divide
To interfere, another time
With Elsie and Papa's Quiet climb!

I got all the things off to Maud & Daisy [Mellen] & am waiting patiently to learn how your Christmas went off.

I am all alone again.

It is charming weather here overhead today — but oh so wet & wretched under feet. I have sent you many articles about the red sunsets, to show you that they seem to prevail all over the world. The best explanation yet is that the earth is passing through some meteoric shower or what might be called cosmic dust. Say an infinite number of infinitely small meteors. The next time you see a flying or shooting star you can imagine something about it. Have you rec the Chart of the Skies I sent you — With love to all — Your loving Papa

The comfortable, homey interior of Glen Eyrie Castle.

(Photos courtesy of Colorado Springs Pioneers Museum)

Marjory Palmer on May 12, 1883
when she was eighteen months old.

(Photo courtesy of Colorado Springs Pioneers Museum)

Dorothy Palmer on her third birthday, October 29, 1883.

(Photo courtesy of Colorado Springs Pioneers Museum)

Queen and Dorothy in 1886.

(Photo courtesy of Colorado Springs Pioneers Museum)

Nevada Avenue, where the cottonwood trees
shipped from Arkansas appear to be flourishing.
(Photo courtesy of Colorado Springs Pioneers Museum)

Cascade Avenue, looking south.
The last building is the Antlers Hotel, c. 1885.
(Photo courtesy of Colorado Springs Pioneers Museum)

CHAPTER FOUR

ENGLAND

In 1883 Queen recognized that she could no longer live in Colorado's thin air. Sleep had become increasingly elusive. It became necessary to spend most of her time in quiet pursuits in her third floor rooms. Her love of books, art, and music helped fill her days, as well as visits from friends, but she was no longer able to enjoy the walking, climbing, and horseback riding at Glen Eyrie.

Her decision to leave Colorado stemmed largely from a desire to regain her health and stamina in order to see her daughters grow into women, but Queen was also concerned about her daughters' education, particularly that of Elsie, who was now eleven years old. Finally she made the decision to move to the East, where she had grown up and still had many friends.

The mother and her three girls, in gypsylike fashion, moved first to Newport, then on to New York. From 1884 to 1886 they lived in the lovely Dakota Hotel at Central Park West and 72nd Street in New York City.

The lower altitude was better for Queen, but the harsh winter weather did not improve her health.

After two winters of illness, Queen and her children moved on to England and its relatively temperate climate. There they spent the next ten years; first in London, then later just southeast of London at Ightham Mote, five miles from Sevenoaks, Kent.

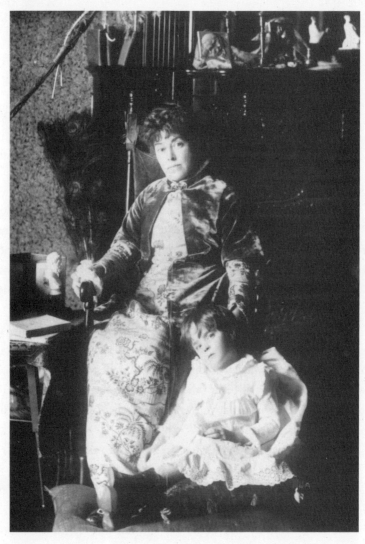

Queen and Marjory while at the Dakota Hotel in
New York City. After two winters of illness in the East,
Queen took her daughters to England.

(Photo courtesy of Colorado Springs Pioneers Museum)

Ightham Mote has been carefully researched and restored by the National Trust of England. The architectural style is of particular interest. The Palmers were tenants of the manor house.

(Photos courtesy of Richard and Robert Culver, Kent, England)

Ightham Mote was a stately manor house built over a period spanning the fourteenth and fifteenth centuries that boasted a gatehouse, great hall, gallery, chapels, large fireplaces, and oak ceilings.

A moat surrounded the house, and a courtyard was contained within. There were beautiful gardens and estate walks. An upper and lower lake originated from an uphill stream and connected to the moat.

Queen made references to the "dearly beloved Mote" where they settled into a quiet English lifestyle.

The Mote — Sept 21

My Dear Will

We have not heard from you for a week and I am not sure whether you are in Glen Eyrie or in New York — but it is a good rule to address letters to New York knowing that they will be forwarded.

I find this place full of the most delicious fruit — so that we wish very often you were here to help us eat it. . . . The peaches are delicious — this is a great thing for the children.

We are beginning to think of winter now — autumn is well upon us — and the Virginia Creeper in the courtyard is glorious in the most vivid red. . . . I got all the list you sent for Glen Eyrie (hair washes & perfume) at Whitelays the other day — although you said to get them at the stores — I could not — as one must pay cash there — and I am sure you will send me the amount as soon as possible.

Katie sails on the 8th (she could not get off sooner because I could not get a cook to replace her sooner) and she will bring all the things sent for — which I hope will reach you safely without delay — I hope you will think it right to pay Katie's passage and fare to Colorado as I explained to you — I thought it was fair to do.

I lay in my winter coal in a day or two and already wood is ready in the wood house, dry and good for the . . . fireplace and the grate.

The babies send love — and Elsie is writing.

Mrs. Frances Wolcott, visiting in England, writes about being invited to dine at Ightham Mote. She was delighted with the swans swimming about the moat as she arrived. The house, however, was not terribly comfortable. She writes:

> *So draughty was that dining-hall that every chair at table had to be screened from drafts from everywhere and nowhere. Our spines were chilled. . . . I know that I felt that a woman's best friend was a hot water bottle and that to jump into bed and pull up the coverlets to shut out sight and sound was but the part of wisdom.*

Queen and Elsie Palmer, 1886
(Photo courtesy of Colorado Springs Pioneers Museum)

The entertainment for the evening, however, was outstanding. A gentleman dressed in a velvet jacket and knee-breeches, wearing patent leather pumps with large ornamental steel buckles, entertained guests with music played on a Stradivarius violin. In spite of the cold, it was an enjoyable evening.

General Palmer was concerned about the cold, damp winters at the Mote and had cabled Queen that she should take the children to the warmer climes of the seashore for the winter months. Queen, concerned about money matters, replied:

Marjory Palmer

(Photo courtesy of Colorado Springs
Pioneers Museum)

Dorothy Palmer

(Photo courtesy of Colorado Springs
Pioneers Museum)

*My Dear Will — Your cable to leave the Mote this season has
come — and I have just replied asking you to "mail me £40 for sea"
which by the time you receive this you will understand from my letter
of the 2nd. I do not want to draw on the £100 you placed for us in
the bank — yet cannot move without money — (you know I pay my
bills for the month before the first of the month — leaving myself very
little cash to go on with till next installment). As soon as I receive the*

£40 we will go — although it almost seems a pity to leave here as a
number of old neighbors have called within the last few days . . . this
place is not damp in the autumn — and the children are in splendid
health — Dorothy especially is fat and her skin now looks brighter
and smoother and healthier than it has ever looked. (I thank Dr.
Morris for the last blessing — what he prescribed for her — has done
wonders.) However I know that a change of air is a good thing now
and then — especially to the sea/from inland and as you seem anxious
too — we will go — as soon as we get the money —

I think we will go to St. Leonards — but have not quite decided
yet — as I want the doctor's opinion as to the place. The only reason
I think of St. Leonards is because I hear through Miss Strettell's Aunt
who lives there that one can get . . . comfortable [accommodations] . . .
near the sea — and I know that it is not so bleak at Eastbourne —

The children are all as happy at their work as possible — Miss
P. certainly has a . . . gift for teaching and lately has been unusu-
ally nice — in all ways. Elsie has never been so interested in her
work — and as for the babies they dance with delight at the mere
thought of going to school . . . Miss P. is most judicious with
them. . . . She never lets them sit more than a few minutes at a time and
varies their lessons with games & marching and jumping about. It is not
so much for what they learn that I have begun this with them — but it
is to get them into powerful habits — and to occupy their minds with
everything that interests them — I do hope my book of Nature will
come soon. It is extraordinary how hard it is to find the right book.

All send love.
Lovingly, Queen

Queen adored her children. Their upbringing was of prime importance to her. She wanted to share with them the qualities and ideals
that were most important to her — loyalty, sincerity, honesty, empa-
thy, a strong sense of duty and responsibility, a love of beauty and

serenity. She still maintained a zest for life, and her infectious enthusiasm spilled over to her girls.

General Palmer made many trips to England, visiting once or twice a year. From Colorado he would write of the beautiful skies and much loved mountains:

> *The weather is warm, quiet and brilliant. Day follows day and night follows night, each surpassing its predecessor, if possible, in beauty. The colouring in the Glen has deepened, and seems so glorious that it is difficult to believe it is true.*

With great anticipation, the girls looked forward to their father's visits. The general brought back the joys, the wildness, the beauty of Glen Eyrie, although for the two younger daughters the memory of that far away land was fading.

Daily life changed dramatically for the girls while he was there with them. Normal routines were forgotten. From raucous games of "circus" to moonlight walks to gaze at the stars, he brought a delicious change. He exploded into their quiet English country living, and they loved it.

General Palmer had many friends in England and many business ventures with them. His visits gave him the opportunity to combine business with pleasure, renewing old friendships, meeting with business associates, and enjoying his family.

From the Mote on July 9th, 1887, Queen wrote:

> *My Dear Will — I have your two letters. . . . Now about my health as regards future plans. I had a thorough examination made by Dr. Sedgwick — the other day — and told him about my house in Colorado — and my desire to get back to it as soon as I am able — He said that in his opinion I should not attempt it for another two years, — (Dr. Fox said the same thing) but he strongly urged my trying Switzerland at once — (because this month is the one*

which would be least trying to me there) . . . going quickly . . . spending a few weeks in the experiment. . . . This he thought would be not only a good thing to do — in order to decide what I would be equal to — but a good change after my year and a half in England — but only for a short time — this he insists upon — So as I have an opportunity of going and being taken care of with Miss Strettell, and the Jamiesons I have decided to go.

Dorothy, left, and Marjory, right. The
Palmer family enjoyed the quiet country
life at the English manor house of Ightham
Mote, near Sevenoaks, Kent.

(Photo courtesy of Colorado Springs Pioneers Museum)

Christmas 1888, was spent at the Mote. Queen included a special note with her gift to sixteen-year-old Elsie. She signed it "Motherling," the affectionate name the children called her:

Ightham Mote, Ivy Hatch, Sevenoaks, Kent
Xmas 88

My Precious daughter — These 6 little hearts are to be worn around your neck, on a delicate little gold chain I shall give you — always. They are meant for Motherling & five other dear friends! You can privately name them — and perhaps tell who they are some day — to your own.

Motherling

Another note from Queen to her eldest daughter illustrates the closeness that developed between them. Written at the Mote, it is simply dated "Friday":

What is there in all this great strange world to be compared to loving one's children! . . . my precious one — you know I have begun to feel you old enough to talk to you — and let you see pain when it is there in Mother's heart — which is yours — now and forever —

Motherling

Their dearly beloved Mote was sold by the owner to Collyer Ferguson on July 31, 1889, and as tenants, the family was given notice to move. It was a wrenching experience to leave their home, as eighteen-year-old Elsie recorded in her journal, March 31, 1890:

Lovely morning. Everything fresh and beautiful. Mother. Little walk before breakfast. After breakfast wandered about and said goodbye. Last place I sat on at the Mote, was the first place I had sat on there: the bench under the little fir tree, looking across the lake to the house with the poplar tree behind. Old Budden [perhaps a gardener] came to say goodbye to Mother. He presented her with some hazelwood canes, saying: "*This* is the Mote." He also brought some blue jays' feathers "for the young ladies." Came away to catch the 11:13 train from Bat & Ball. Since then have been in a dream.

The family moved several more times. Leaving the Mote at Sevenoaks, they moved to Blackdown, where they lived from April 1 to September 31, 1890. The house, which dated from 1640, was two miles south of Hazelmere in Surrey.

The Oak Cottage in Frant, Sussex, was their next residence. Elsie tells about it in her diary, dated November 1, 1890: "Went with Miss L. & Dos [Dorothy] to Frant, where we have rented a cottage, until the right house turns up. A very pretty little place; my room lovely."

By April, 20, 1892, a "graceful, Elizabethan" house at Loseley, Guildford was located. It was southwest of London and fulfilled Queen's quest for quiet country living. Elsie writes in her diary:

Today Mother & I moved into Loseley. The children are at Saxonbury [Saxonbury Lodge, Frant, where architect, Fred Jamieson, lived. He was supervising alterations at Loseley] for another week until the house is more in order. Helen Mellen & Fred came with us. Fred very busy with the workmen. . . . At present the dining room and my future bed-room are in the greatest state of confusion. . . . Felt a little badly at leaving the dear cottage. But can hardly believe that we have at last got here to stay.

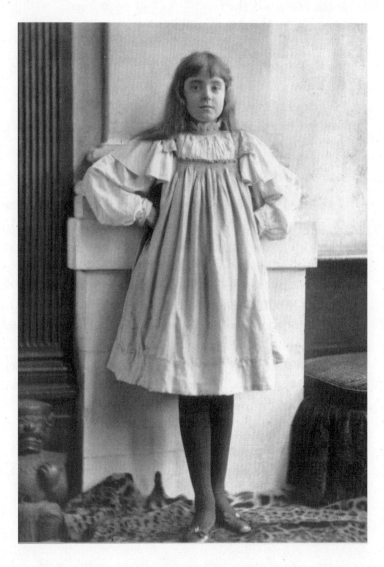

Marjory Palmer, 1892
(Photo courtesy of Colorado Springs Pioneers Museum)

Dorothy Palmer, 1892
(Photo courtesy of Colorado Springs Pioneers Museum)

They were not to stay, however, and eventually moved back to Oak Cottage in Frant. Marshall Sprague explains in *Newport in the Rockies*:

> As in 1876, when he had closed Glen Eyrie briefly to live on Cascade Avenue, Palmer cut his personal expenses, and these included the separate establishment in England of his wife Queen and their daughters, Elsie, Dorothy, and Marjory. Since the 1880's, Palmer had maintained for Queen a large place in Loseley Park, Guildford, Surrey, where she had entertained literary and artistic people like the widowed novelist, George Meredith, and the young American painter, John Singer Sargent. In the summer of '93 Palmer was in England arranging for Queen and the girls to give up Loseley Park. In its place, they took a cottage at Frant, Sussex.

Queen and William shared a passion for travel. They first met on a moving train headed west. They traveled across an ocean on their honeymoon, and later experienced the eventful trip to Mexico together. William, it seemed, never tired of the travel that his successful railroad demanded, and the entire family journeyed to the East and to Europe several times.

Queen's failing health was restrictive, but in 1889 she and William traveled to France and Italy. It was a dream trip for Queen, who had studied and enjoyed the arts throughout her life. The opportunity to see the original masterpieces that she loved and the historic architecture of Europe was indeed a dream come true.

The children were left at home, although several companions accompanied the Palmers. Alma Strettell, who had been visiting in Colorado when Queen suffered her first heart attack, was among them.

Queen kept a daily journal of her trip. and filled it with keen observations and vivid descriptions. Her conservative background is apparent in her writing.

Queen and William, and their companions, left the Mote and the children on March 8, 1889, in the rain, "Reached Tonbridge Station in plenty of time. . . . Reached Dover 1 1/2 hours too early for boat—Employ time in writing to Elsie, and eating Fry's dainty sandwiches, and in looking at Illustrated News."

Sailing on a vessel named the *Empress*, Queen observed her fellow passengers and noted:

> Passengers more or less interesting—Vulgar couple near us—but girl has strange fascinating eyes—It struck me as I looked at her lying back languidly in her chair—how a pretty face may conceal its vulgarity—if it *is* vulgar—until it speaks or smiles—when one wishes it hadn't! Just as refinement, without beauty—is often not detected until it speaks or smiles.
>
> Calais reached—after a pretty good crossing. Sent children telegram and take places in carriage for Paris with 5 other ladies—all of whom become *intimate* in an hour! I bury myself in New "American" with an occasional interruption when something is too good not to share it with P. [Palmer] who *always* understands. . . . What a difference the little belt of water makes! We are in quite a different atmosphere and country—where, from the sky—(at this moment a lovely blue) to the very *rubbish heaps*—there is difference, subtle—but real and indescribable—the trees are so different, too—and (ah Yes!) the people. Reached Paris 7:50—Custom house . . . at the end of a rather fatiguing day—but we are finally packed into our little omnibus—and rattle off through the

interminable Rue Lafayette (which "strange to say," reminds me of Broadway!) and in 30 minutes reach our nice little Hotel Meyerbeer—I begin to feel that I am really traveling. P. in order to save me stairs has engaged rooms [on lower level] but we will not do that again—as the ceilings are so very low. Clean comfortable place—I luxuriate.

Paris—Saturday March 9—Fine bright morning—after rather a sultry night—hot coffee & rolls—(delicious foreign place!) make one forget it. And we go forth in holiday spirits—at first the sun shines—and the beautiful Place de la Concorde—no wonder the Parisiennes are proud . . . it is splendid in the sun as we drive gaily through it. But presently it begins to pour—However we are independent of weather . . . we drive on (not to the "Louvre"—as we *should*) to the Maison de louvre—and we are held by its charm, in enthusiastic admiration for more than an hour! Gowns, scarfs . . . skirts, gloves, boots, lingerie—all appeal to our eyes, which have fasted upon English solidity for so long. Filled with remorse for having given way to this frivolous impulse we rush from the shop to throw ourselves into the open . . . arms of Art—and are driven quickly to a water color exhibition.

In Paris they were invited to dinner by an acquaintance, Miss Roubelle, described by Queen:

Tall, thin, pale, fair, American accent, original, good-hearted, forty-five . . . gave us the pleasant society and a charming little dinner in her pretty apartment, up many flights of stairs—I had my first experience at being carried in the chair P. got for me — and it was a success (it is to be hoped that the shrinking from physical dependence will soon be gone!). On to a play at the Francais — good play — every part well filled.

The chair is not mentioned again but undoubtedly the conveyance allowed Queen to do things that would have been physically impossible otherwise. William's loving effort to assist his wife is touching.

Sunday March 10, train to Avignon — P. Paid bill, thinking it too much, exhausting trip but went on a walking tour of Avignon with intelligent guide, streets lined with picturesque houses to a 14th century cathedral adjoining a palace — these buildings are both very massive — and the palace has a prison like look. The stone of which they are built (as wide as the 39 towers which are formed on the wall of the tower) is a light brown, rather than grey, I should say — which relieved it of the cold look that some grey gives a massive and unornamented building — the cathedral is very interesting — and looked beautiful in the sun. An almond tree, the first I had seen, was in full bloom against the grim walls — This gave me a shock of pleasure . . . the cathedral has some old frescoes by Simone Memmi — but they are too faded to see well. . . . It has also rather an interesting cupola, very unusual, I think. We are told that Laura lived at Avignon — and that Petrarcho saw her first here.

Leaving this area they continued on their walk:

We dropped steeply down from the hill and walked along the bank of the river, where picturesque boats laden with red and golden apples gave a vivid color to the scene . . . and so to our hotel. After breakfast we pay our bill (again too much P. says).

They "determined to come back with some of our friends who will appreciate it, some day." Queen described the scenery seen from the train, "We pass great orchards of almond trees, in full bloom, which are particularly beautiful scattered about among the grey olives, whose leaves glitter in the sunshine like silver."

The next stop, Marseilles, she found "full of busy people" with an intense "air of business":

> What a dreary place it is, Marseilles, and how ugly it is — we think as we drive home — although we first drive down to the port to see ships which certainly is a fine sight. After our two hours drive we go back to the hotel, to dinner ("bouillabaisse" the dish of Marseilles, consisting of all kinds of fish boiled together and made into soup). I believe my mattress is made of india rubber — it's so firm that tired as I am, I almost laugh myself to sleep!

The Palmers visited the museum to see the frescoes and the picture gallery, which "except for a pretty Perugrino and a doubtful Corot was most amusingly wretched." They left by train and found the time was shortened by the interesting acquaintance of a famous stage actor. The journey took them into Italy, and at each stop Queen was delighted to receive letters from home, and anxious when there was none. "I read R. Ellsmere to P. until bedtime," she writes.

> Saturday, March 16 — Italy — The view I get early from the window is very beautiful. The sea is still as a lake and the Estuels are clothed in an opal light — pale and soft in the distance.

About Duria Castle she muses:

I wish I could give an idea of the wonderful effect of light and color—with the sparkling brilliancy of the atmosphere, and the delicious feeling of . . . light and air. The day was certainly perfect and individual—in that it was unlike any other fine day elsewhere. It had some of the quality of Colorado air, just as the scenery was dimly suggestive of Colorado.

We got back rather tired—but so repaid—for I have pictures to keep in my memory forever. . . . Shall sleep sweetly tonight.

Monday—March 18—Another perfect day! I sent off some tiny oranges—to my babies and to my Daisy—and then we drive down to the old town of Bordijhera—What a lovely, old place. It is like one great house—with many corridors—narrow, and winding —like a labyrinth—with now and then a surprizing [sic] peep through the low arches of sea and sky & great green palms & olives. The open Plaza—is most charming. The friendly open church—invites one to wander in—where one may say one's little prayer. In the afternoon we drive to the Valle Crosia. We went past several of the characteristic Italian villages which I am becoming delightedly familiar with. I take much pleasure in the straight back cypress trees—they are so full of—can I say dignity and also give a style to the hill sides.

Monte Carlo and Monaco were the next destination for the Palmers, who traveled there by carriage:

> We reach Monte Carlo having discussed the question of gambling—and decided that we will do *nothing* except look at the players—We drive into town—take our breakfast at a café near the Casino (Café Riche) and then go into the big ugly building which *sprawls* on a good deal of ground. And which is built in a vulgar showy manner. We then go into a big marble room—with dark marble pillars and mosaic floors—through which we pass into the first of the gambling rooms—where there are two tables for "Roulette"—we watch this for a time—and notice the hard depraved faces of the players—very quiet and showing no excitement. Their piles of gold and bank notes lie in little heaps before them—and although their eyes are . . . watchful one could not detect any other sign of excitement. The money rattles—and the croupiers pull it in with their rakes—and throw it out again—and the horrid game goes on—for it is *repulsive* to me—although I have thought that it might have some attraction. . . . How could I have thought it possible that I should have found a remote desire to "put down" anything on the tables? We go on to another room—bigger but darker—then into the third and last where all the light of day is closed out by closely drawn . . . curtains and they are playing *by lamplight*!
>
> There is one pretty girl—not more than 18 or 20—who has a great pile of gold and notes before her. Sitting next to her is an old man—who seems to be advising her—but who is playing too. She has a determined face—which is not even flushed with her acknowledged

success—for she has evidently been winning largely. An older—but still young woman—seems to be playing against her . . . we don't wait for the result—it has become too painful—it reminds one strangely of a tropical growth of parasites. We walked . . . overlooking the lovely bays—and I soon become soothed and sane again. We took the fiacre to Monaco.

On to San Remo and Genoa: The hills are more picturesque in outline and are more "fold on fold"—than I have yet seen. The place is most picturesque and the wide piazzas . . . tantalizing glimpses through the big gateways as we drive along—helps to make us realize that we are indeed in the country of warmth and sun—We reach our hotel (du Park) at 6:30 and after a glance at our room . . . we decide that we will not remain there more than one night (it is dark and disagreeable). We go for our table d'hôte dinner (letters from home). Rosiana comes—a dear dignified soul—and beautiful with the face of a Mater Dolorosa—splendid melancholy eyes—and sweet soft voice and gesture. I am quite impressed by her—We go to bed early—I find myself more tired than I have been.

In Genoa, Queen says:

The cathedral of San Lorenzo, surprisingly beautiful (having driven past P.'s old apartments.) — "the first black and white" marble church I have seen . . . and to my own surprise I like it—but what I like best is the whole front of the building—which has three beautiful doorways . . . having been built in the 12th and 13th centuries . . . the interior of the church looks to belong to a quite different period. . . . I am delighted with the gardens—covered with creepers, which they have on many of the roofs—we drive about looking at the many picturesque streets (often festooned with the week's washing!) and there to the Zerbino garden—which is wide and lovely—and from which one gets lovely views of Genoa—following the curve of the lovely bay . . . and the promontories beyond—among which is Portofino. We go . . . to see "Amleto" (Hamlet) by the great Duse as we think . . . but we find a very amusing . . . Hamlet full of useless vehement emotion (generally writhing on the floor and looking for his father's ghost—as he would look for a pin on the floor—and a most amusing wooden Ophelia—in a blue cotton gown—fastened with white buttons and short in front with petticoat showing—voluminous skirts, etc.—we put away in the middle of one of their acts—and draw a sigh of relief when we are safely in our carriage—although we have had an amusing evening.

March 27, Wednesday—Florence: I get up at 4:30 to throw open my shutters—to let in the light and to get a daylight glimpse of this wonderful City—which is so full of promised delight. . . . (P. and I have separate though communicating rooms—which is much pleasanter—as we can each indulge our little eccentricities without disturbing the other!) For more than an hour—listening to the early sounds—bells, clocks, and donkeys (!) until I find myself stiff & cold—and need to find bed and warmth again.—But I am too excited to sleep any more—so at 7 I dress—Lee comes at 8—and is amazed to find I have fled! And go to get coffee—and hastening to rush out—but know I mustn't till P. is ready. We drive first through the Piazza della Signorina.

Queen is excited to see San Marco — the church, the monastery, and the cloisters. The monastery is rich in frescoes, each monk's cell had a fresco by Fra Angelico. In another small chapel nearby she falls in love with a fresco of "The daughter of Herodias dancing before Herod" and a symbolic figure of Faith — "I wish I could express how these things satisfied me!"

> Florence — March 29, Thursday — I must begin my day's account by saying that I am *almost wild with delight!!!* A new hunger is discovered in me — by myself which has been gradually growing — ever since I left Nice — and it has reached its climax in this great — beautiful Florence. . . . I am almost wild with the joy of living and seeing and healthy in this air — saturated with the beauty of the past and present.

Queen's lifelong dream of seeing the paintings and sculptures of the Renaissance artists of Italy became reality. For her Botticelli, Donatello, Michelangelo, and Raphael came to life.

Later in 1889 General Palmer took Elsie on an extended trip to Switzerland. Together, the father and daughter traveled, from August 17 to October 5, further forging the close relationship that lasted throughout their lives.

In March of 1891 Queen and Elsie, now nineteen, went to Paris together. Perhaps it was a shopping trip.

In the summer of 1893, from their home in Loseley, Queen journeyed, with her daughters, to Germany and Scotland. Elsie was a young lady of twenty-one. Dorothy was thirteen and Marjory twelve.

It was a wonderful summer for the children and especially memorable. Their mother insisted that they keep a journal to record new experiences. Time was set aside each day for their journal writing. They also wrote to their father, in Colorado, and to Tante, who was perhaps a favorite governess or nanny, who remained in England. Traveling by omnibus they went to London, then by train to Edinburgh.

It is apparent from the journals that Queen's younger daughters had been sheltered and protected. They found enjoyment in new experiences and simple amusements.

Dorothy, who was called Dos, tells of going to pick out some pretty plaids: "We all three are going to have caps made out of the plads [sic] called the Royal Sturt [sic], the hunting Sturt and the dress Sturt. We saw some soldiers with very pretty kilts."

The younger girls learned to skip stones in the lochs, two, three, and four times and they were very impressed with a gentleman who was able to make them skip ten times. They rode horses, being careful of the bogs, Marjory wrote, "because they looked just like moss." It was great fun for these proper young ladies to be allowed to discard shoes and stockings and run down the road barefoot. A highlight of each day was tea time, when their mother read to them from a favorite book.

Reading was an important part of their growing up and Dorothy was quite impressed when she and her mother "went to the Reading room and got *Dombey and Son* also two other books. It caustes [sic] a peny [sic] a day to have them, but on Sundays it does not causte anything. In the afternoon we read *Dombey and Son* together."

A childish highlight of the summer seemed to be a game the young girls devised with billiard balls. Sailing little boats also was a favorite pastime, "It was so nice to see the little breachers [waves] (for unless it is a very rough day, there are no breachers) always bring them back."

Living in England improved Queen's general health, but the heart problems continued to plague her. She was very afraid that her children would be left without her. In July 1886, she wrote a letter to them, hoping that they would never need to read it:

July 1886

My Precious three little girls — Mother wants to be very sure that you have some words from her — for "God Speed" — in case she should be called away suddenly on a long journey without time to speak them to you before she goes — Sweethearts — you will listen to them I know and will remember them for her sake — who loves you always — better than life.

First of all — Be true — my darlings — search always untiringly for that truth. . . . Let falsehood be finally painful to you.

Be kind — Be Kind — Be Kind — As you do not know how much a kind word or act may do for one who may need it — Mother thinks that kindness is more beautiful than any virtue you may have.

Be gentle — and brave — with a hand always outstretched to any soul who may be helped by it — and as you freely give be generous to receive — don't feel that the privilege — (great indeed though it may be and is!) of giving belongs to you exclusively.

Elsie — you know how much we have talked of your being the little mother of the other two. Think of that now — my first born — my precious daughter — I need say no more to your loving soul than never forget — that Motherling is near you, blessing you — always — forever — helping you — comforting you — and waiting for you and your baby sisters — those other two that we love so dearly. Make them brave and good — kind and true — as you will be. And let them know how "Motherling" is loving them — and near them. You will read these words to them — so that they will remember what Mother said to them — and you will show them by your own sweet love how mother loved them — loves you all — better than all the world besides —

You will not be sad but bright and happy with them. Mother is resting (you know how tired she often was — my darling) and happy,

*and glad in your joys, and goodness. And you will have work to do,
my daughters — and you will let the world be much better that you
have lived in it.*

*You do not need Motherling to say more to you — your own
hearts will beat with hers — and will understand each other always.*

*With an everlasting kiss from your precious lips — my three own
babies, my own, own ones — I say to you — for Motherling is with
you — forever — only you don't see her — you will remember — how
she loves you.*

Your Motherling — God be with you.

Four years later, Queen reviewed her letter, grateful for the additional time she had with her daughters. She added a special note to Elsie:

March 28th, 1890
Ightham Mote, Ivy Hatch, Sevenoaks, Kent

*If I should write farewell words to you now — they would be the
same. Darling — since writing them we have had four full, precious
years (more than I ever hoped for) — with my treasures. Perhaps you
will never see the words I have written — for I am stronger — not
so tired any more and even though we are on the eve of leaving our
beloved Mote — I am happy. We have had so many sweet, close
talks — you know so well — My Little companion — how mother
feels about little and great things! It is a comfort always, to know
that even if I should go to sleep tonight — not to wake again in
this world — I have been able to go so far on your journey with
you — and the little ones. What a joy it is.*

A draft of a letter from Queen to William begs him to consider living in England with her. It is not known if the letter was ever sent to him or, if it was, what response might have been made. The year that she wrote it is uncertain. The date is September 20:

And now, my dear Will about my health — and prospect of being able to live in America. I gave you the opinion of the three physicians who know my trouble best. When I wrote to you a few months ago — and nothing has happened since to change their opinion. — That New York is on a level with the sea is quite true — but the strain of the climate even there might be fatal for me at present. The very thing in this English climate which is called relaxing to some people — is the quality most favorable for my condition which as I think I wrote you — is more sensitive for the next few years ["seven or eight" are crossed out] than it will be afterward. If the children were older — I should not hesitate to try — notwithstanding their opinions for I might do well enough and if I did not — it wouldn't make so much difference but as it is — I want to see them grown up — if possible. . . . But, I will not let you be so homeless any more — if you cannot come to us — Elsie must make a home for you there. You know how decidedly fond of you she is.

Is it quite impossible for you to come to England? — with only an occasional visit to America? Can you not give up some of your responsibilities there — and with a smaller income in consequence — be happy with your little family here? I should look for a house a little larger than this — in a beautiful part of the country — where we could all be so happy together — and then — after a few years that I ought to remain here — we might all be able to go back to our own home in Glen Eyrie, for the doctors say that after these years, if I get well enough with them I will be better than I have been since that attack of bronchitis in New York. . . . Do consider this well — it would be a rest and change for you, too, that would probably do you good, as well. If you say so — I could look about and find our little house and be all ready for you when you come next.

Elsie Palmer, the eldest daughter, returned to America for a visit after an absence of ten years. How things had changed! Her father's luxurious private railroad car was waiting for them in New York, complete with servants and secretary as William's wealthy status allowed. They leisurely traveled together through the south, then across the plains and into the mountains that she had never forgotten. At night the "Nomad" was switched onto a siding so that no part of the exciting and changing scenery would be missed.

At Glen Eyrie she was welcomed by the dogs, the horses, the servants, and many old friends. It was a special time for Elsie and her father.

She returned to England in September. As Christmas approached, her mother was very ill, confining herself to her rooms so that her daughters would not see how much she suffered. On Christmas Day, Elsie, now twenty-two, wrote a note to her mother, who lay upstairs:

Xmas 1894
Oak Cottage, Frant, Sussex

Good Morning — my own darling Motherling, I can write you — now — though I can't talk to you because it tires you. It was a splendid stocking! And the dress doesn't need a single alteration. I wonder if you think we are not having a happy Xmas — because we are — dearest Motherling — and we feel your presence with us every second. It's wonderful how you do that! And all your little thoughts for people's pleasure — come showering downstairs to every one, and are kept close all the time — almost as if you were there. The present is not quite finished — as I think you will like it better with a certain trimming I have for it.

Your own Elsie

When news of Queen's last illness was received by General Palmer, he left immediately for Oak Cottage in Frant to be at her side. William traveled by train to New York and engaged the first available steamer sailing to England. Sadly, however, he did not reach her in time. Death came on December 27, 1894. She was forty-four years old. Queen and William had been married twenty-four years.

Elsie's journal entry simply says, "Mother died today."

Left to right, Dorothy, Queen, and Marjory; Elsie, third from right, 1893, at Ightham Mote.
(Photo courtesy of Colorado Springs Pioneers Museum)

CHAPTER FIVE

MEMORIES

Historians' opinions vary about the length of time Queen spent in Colorado. Marshall Sprague in his *Newport in the Rockies* seems to feel that Queen did not make a serious effort to accept Glen Eyrie and Colorado Springs, making only sporadic visits in 1874, 1878, and 1880. F. C. Thornton, on the other hand, reports that Queen lived quietly at Glen Eyrie after the heart trouble began that eventually was the cause of her death. She spent more time in the spacious third floor rooms with books and music. Thornton's account of Queen reports that she fought against her illness for five years before leaving the home she dearly loved. Sleep had become virtually impossible at the high altitude.

On December 31, 1894, the following appeared in the Colorado Springs Woman's Edition of the *Evening Telegraph:*

> The last days of the year are saddened by the news . . . from across the sea of the death of one who in days gone by filled a leading place in our little community and it is most fitting that a lasting and respectful tribute should be made to her memory. Mrs. Palmer was identified with the earliest history of our City. While living among us, she was always closely connected with social life and deeply interested in the development of the City.

We all remember the graceful hospitality, so generously offered in her unique home at Glen Eyrie; the charms that made her preeminently a leader in society; her ready sympathy for the artistic whether in music, literature or art; her appreciation of beauty in nature and her almost worship of the true and beautiful wherever found, as well as her quick detection and intense dislike of the untrue. With main attractions of mind and person, her strong characteristic was faithfulness to friends.

No one more fully understood and answered the demands of friendship with more grace and satisfaction than Mrs. Palmer. A loving, devoted and judicious mother, a wise and charming presider over her household, our tender sympathy goes out to those who are bereaved of her gentle guidance and beautiful presence. E. R. R.

In the obituary printed in the January 3, 1895, edition of the Colorado Springs *Gazette Telegraph* it states, in part:

From the beginning Mrs. Palmer was the leader in the educational and social life of the place [Colorado Springs]. She established the first school, teaching it herself, pro bono publico, in the house at the corner north of and opposite the old high school on Cascade avenue, until a district could be organized and its revenues established.

Her death will be deplored by many friends in this city to whom the news comes as a great shock.

Her illness was attributed to "a trouble of the valve of the heart." Other writers have surmised that she suffered from rheumatic heart disease.

The Fifty-First Annual Edition of the Colorado Springs *Gazette Telegraph,* dated April 8, 1923, devoted considerable space to "Mrs. Palmer's Splended Part in City's Building." The article was written by her friend, F. C. Thornton:

BECAME MOVING SPIRIT IN COLONY

It is by our struggles that we rise. No one can understand Mrs. Palmer, nee Queen Mellen, who does not realize what she had to fight against. Fancy a willful beauty, with such a given name as "Queen", and brought up to despise self-control.

Endowed far above the average with what makes a woman irresistible, all felt that her natural setting was the whirl and possibilities of a brilliant social life in one of the older cities. There were, however, as all who knew her well in later days could see, finer qualities underneath that made her choose a life which at least for years was the antithesis of the one for which she seemed best fitted; just as we all felt she herself, on the face of it, was the antithesis of her soldier husband, nearly 16 years her senior. A man who had never been given a chance to study women at close range, or indeed to enjoy the amenities which belonged to social circles of people of elegant leisure, rather than of strenuous achievement. A man already absorbed in developing new countries by the building of railroads and founding of cities with that indomitable persistence and absorption which was the foundation of his remarkable war record.

This was the girl who left behind her all for which she seemed so eminently fitted to come to an unsettled country as hostess for her husband's friends and, as she was bound to become, the moving spirit of the little village of Colorado Springs that stood where now our modern city stands; she helped to build the first church; no case of suffering escaped her. . . .

KEPT COLONISTS IN GOOD SPIRIT

Thru the first years of stagnation which followed the excitement of the first boom, the visions of a glorious future began to fade away before the hardship and monotony of those early days. It was sympathy for this reaction which caused her to give her most valuable contribution to the welfare of the village. She spent her time in devising any and every kind of amusement that she could think of to help drive away the blues, and as her reward won the devotion and love of all.

As the town developed and there was more to help, her personal activities in the village lessened. . . . I have always remembered as a wonderful example of her irresistible leadership, which she always achieved without a touch of the dominating personality.

Our splendid young woman, Mrs. Palmer, was more than equal to doing the great lady of the district and to being the hospitable hostess of Glen Eyrie to which haven all were invited. She threw all her faculties as well as her charms into her efforts to make Glen Eyrie the most charming home in the region, if not in the world, with such success as to earn the gratitude and admiration of her husband. This being done in spite of the fact that she had a string of admirers in attendance at all times.

IN THE DAYS OF ILL FORTUNE

As is inevitable in a new country, clouds came eventually, and bad financial days. To me one of the most beautiful thoughts about her, which I shall carry to my grave, was that even when they became really poor, she was the same beautiful enthusiast, if anything more vivid than in the days of her prosperity.

When I married she extended her gracious hospitality to my wife when I first brought her to Colorado Springs. They were living at that time in quite a small house, or rather half a house, on Cascade Avenue, to which they had come because they were too poor to keep open their beloved home at Glen Eyrie. I never knew her more charming and beautifully natural than she was in those very restricted surroundings, especially so in contrast with the luxuries of Glen Eyrie.

With care and economy, that particular storm was averted and they had been back in Glen Eyrie for some years when the worst time in the history of the Denver and Rio Grande railroad occurred.

The ways of all pioneer promoters are hard, but when a pioneer throws his whole personal fortune into the welfare of every undertaking he fathers, those ways are indescribably hard, and I know of nothing in Mrs. Palmer's life that proved her strength of purpose and loyalty better than her behavior at that time.

The battle with their old enemy, the powerful Santa Fe organization, had driven the little road to the very last ditch. Matters looked desperate and General Palmer, the one to whom all looked for safety, took his responsibility with desperate seriousness. So much so that his bodily health was giving way under the strain. Mrs. Palmer knew that he was sick and also knew that the strain was more than he could possibly bear unless he got a rest once in a while; and so she tried all the time to get him to take a day or two off now and then. She never left his side and they were alone in Glen Eyrie, the

children having been sent off to Manitou Park to spend
the summer.

A WOMAN OF INDOMITABLE WILL

One Saturday, she succeeded in persuading him to take
a horseback ride in Manitou Park where the children
were, which he did with understanding that she should
come with him. They met a bad wind storm about where
Green Mountain Falls now stands. The wind was bad
enough to carry considerable gravel. No mean fight for
a young woman who had always hated wind . . . she
persisted in fighting on their way until at last seeing
close by the track, a heavy bush where she might get
shelter, she slid to the ground, calling to her husband,
"Give me just five minutes, and I promise you that I will
be all right."

As she told us all, laughingly, when they eventually reached the hotel, "I tell you I made the best use of
my rest. I was in a furious passion, as if the wind were
a person, so I lay kicking and screaming, as if I were
crazy."

At the end of five minutes, the General said that
she mounted her horse and led the struggle thru the
storm until they reached a ranch house close to where
Woodland Park is today, where they waited until the
storm abated.

I would not have told this intimate incident if it did
not show her indomitable will which could overcome
even her temperamental drawbacks.

It was to give a true picture of a splendidly capable
and fascinating woman . . . and felt sure that she would
like others to know her as she really was.

FORCED TO GO TO ENGLAND

Her life, alas! was to be a short one. The beginning of the heart trouble that eventually brought death began to show themselves before she had been 10 years in Colorado. And tho she fought against pain and sleeplessness for nearly five years more, her activities were lessened and she had to live as quietly as possible at Glen Eyrie, which they had improved wonderfully after the fight had been won and they had escaped the clutches of the Santa Fe.

Eventually she had to give up the fight and leave her home of which she was passionately fond because sleep became impossible at this altitude. For a time she became more or less of a wanderer among her friends in the east, but General Palmer eventually took her to England, to which place he had very often made trips because a number of his financial friends lived there and in Belgium. In England she had a small circle of friends, mostly made originally in Glen Eyrie, with whom she was happy. After a few years she died unexpectedly, after about a month's intense suffering, the latter part of which time she separated herself from her children rather than let them suffer at the sight of her agony. A splendid ending to a short life, full of splendid good times as well as earnest efforts at real things, which she accomplished in spite of temperamental as well as early environmental difficulties.

Again in 1926 the August 1 issue of the Colorado Springs Sunday *Gazette Telegraph* paid tribute to Queen.

MRS. PALMER BIG FACTOR IN EARLY DAYS,
Organized First Church, Aided Unfortunate, Named
Streets:

Colorado Springs will always remember Gen.
William J. Palmer, founder of the city. And it will never
forget Mrs. Palmer.

It is told of how Queens canon [canyon] was named
for Mrs. Palmer, whom her husband called Queen,
because he thought it the most beautiful of canons in
the region.

Mrs. Palmer it was who named many of the other
places of the Pikes Peak region. The west was open like
a new paradise just unfolded. There were attractions
hereabouts at every turn. But they were nameless. Mrs.
Palmer had a talent for applying names to them and it is
told that she greatly enjoyed doing so.

Besides this she taught school and in many ways
aided in a manner that makes her memory lovable in
settling the new community.

The article again quoted F. C. Thornton:

Mrs. Palmer's great charm was her mental sparkle, the
suggestion of which, I think, as well as that of unfailing kindness, can be clearly seen. . . . One of the most
beautiful things that can be said of her is that she was
never known to say an unkind or sarcastic word of
anyone, absent or present. To me, however, her greatest
charm was her dread of sham and show. Whatever her
financial resources were at the time, her love of dress
was invariably governed by her artistic taste. With her
there could be no pleasure in any effort at adornment
which contained even a speck of the advertising element.

This conviction was so strong that it made her refuse to wear costly jewels, though she reveled in their color and freely used semi-precious stones, and even really beautiful artistic efforts in glass. All this in spite of constant attacks from friends who felt that her style of beauty demanded diamonds, emeralds and rubies. When I tell you that the charms which I have tried to picture were capped by a wonderful mezzo voice, which she could use for overwhelming interpretations, can anyone wonder that men were her devoted slaves, and such women as understood her, loved her to distraction.

Elsie, Dorothy, and Marjory came home to the castle in Colorado after their mother's death.

It was not until 1903–1904, well after Queen's death, that wealthy, retired General Palmer transformed Glen Eyrie into the impressive stone castle that is in existence today. Mr. Sterner, architect and builder, perpetuated Queen's original ideas and the characteristics of the original structure.

Stones were quarried in nearby Bear Creek Canyon. When the core of the house, the beehive structure of Queen's design, was surrounded by the stone, the original wood frame was removed.

Rhoda Davis Wilcox, author of *The Man on the Iron Horse* described the new Glen Eyrie:

There were over sixty-five rooms in the castle, with a drawing room for the ladies, a library, a den, and a large dining hall. The kitchen and butler's pantry shone with white tile walls and blue and white floors and there were special rooms for the silverware and for flower arranging. There were turkish baths and servants quarters, a milk room for the dairy maids, and a special ice room filled with ice-making machinery. On top of the tower was a roof garden where a large bell of silver alloy was hung. The bell, made in Germany, weighed a ton and rang with a powerful tone which could be heard for six miles.

William survived his Queen by fifteen years. His death occurred on March 13, 1909.

A town with beauty and grace, Colorado Springs evolved from the dusty frontier camp of the 1870's just as Gen. Palmer had envisioned.

(Photo courtesy of Pikes Peak Library District, Local History Collection)

View from the Bijou Bridge, c. 1900. The fledgling pioneer
town had come a long way.

(Photo courtesy of Colorado Springs Pioneers Museum)

Tejon Street, looking south, c. 1900.
Power poles and tall trees lined the busy downtown streets.

(Photo courtesy of Colorado Springs Pioneers Museum)

Eighteen months after William's death Queen's ashes were disinterred from an English graveyard and placed near the General's under a smaller Ute Pass stone. Together again, William and his Queen rest now in the Palmers' raised plot in Evergreen Cemetery, Colorado Springs, Colorado.

AFTERWORD: GLEN EYRIE SINCE 1894

After General Palmer's death in 1909, his daughters offered the estate to the city of Colorado Springs, but it proved too expensive to maintain and was sold in 1916 to a group of Oklahoma businessmen who called themselves the Glen Eyrie Companies. They paid $150,000 for the property, planning to use it as a private resort and country club, complete with an eighteen-hole golf course. The carriage house became The Black Horse Tavern (the name probably taken from General Palmer's black horse Señor). The castle was to be used as the clubhouse, and the glen was in fact plotted into 150 luxury home sites.

But World War I was at its height, and people were not interested in the cost of maintaining a home at a private country club. Faced with the lack of sales, the owners of the Glen Eyrie Companies were delighted with an offer from multimillionaire rug manufacturer Alexander Smith Cochran to purchase the estate for $450,000. Cochran also purchased the Douglas, Lansing, Austin, Newton, and Fairley Ranches north of Glen Eyrie.

In 1925, Cochran built a separate residence on the property, known as the Pink House, and closed the castle. Just two years later, in August 1927, the estate was put up for auction in two parcels. For parcel one, Glen Eyrie and the ranchland to the south, the bid was

$250,000. Parcel two included the ranchland to the north and garnered a bid of $50,000. The high bidder was Harold Lumberg, a New York attorney. Lumberg failed to close within the sixty days allowed, however, and the estate remained with Cochran's holding company, the Hillbright Corporation.

Cochran died in 1929, and Glen Eyrie remained on the market until 1938, when it was purchased by George W. Strake, an independent oil man from Houston, Texas. He used Glen Eyrie as a summer home and cattle ranch. He added two wings to the Pink House, where his family lived while at Glen Eyrie. In 1950 the estate again was placed on the market, this time for $500,000.

In 1953 a Colorado Springs real estate broker contacted Billy Graham about the Glen Eyrie estate, knowing that Graham was looking for a headquarters for his ministry. When Mr. Strake heard that Graham was considering the property, he lowered the price to $300,000, plus $40,000 for furnishings.

Dawson Trotman, founder of the Navigators, saw the property and told Graham, "If you don't want Glen Eyrie, The Navigators do." At first Graham wanted to purchase the property and have The Navigators headquarter at Glen Eyrie and maintain it, as Trotman's organization had taken over responsibility for counselor training and follow-up for Graham's own Billy Graham Crusades. But later Graham withdrew from the negotiations with the provision that The Navigators would take over the option to purchase the estate.

At the time, the fledgling Navigators had no money and no benefactors. Miraculously, however, they raised a down payment of $110,000 in six weeks, with the average donation being twenty dollars. As a last gesture of good will, George Strake included more than three hundred acres adjoining the mountain reservoir at the head of Queen's Canyon. This property is now used by The Navigators for Eagle Lake Camp.

Billy Graham said it all when he exclaimed, "God did it!" The way was now open for the fulfillment of Trotman's fourfold vision for the property. It has since become the home of the international headquarters for The Navigators, the site of a year-round training program, a conference center, and a place for Christian leaders of other organizations to gather for fellowship and prayer.

Since 1953 the peaceful and beautiful grounds have served as a place of rest and rejuvenation, a reminder of the importance of stillness and prayer in service to God. The conferences and training programs held on the grounds throughout the year motivate and reenergize attendees with knowledge of God's truth and love. Both aspects of the Glen Eyrie ministry, the property and the programs, perfectly align with and enrich the mission of The Navigators: to know Christ and make Him known.

BIBLIOGRAPHY

Fisher, John D. *Builder of the West*. Caldwell, ID: Caxton Printers, 1939.

The Flushing Journal. Flushing, NY, November 19, 1870. Courtesy of The Queens Borough Public Library, Long Island Division.

Howbert, Irving. *Memories of a Lifetime in the Pikes Peak Region*. New York: Putnam, 1925.

Kingsley, Rose. *South by West*. London: W. Isbister & Co., 1874.

"Mrs. Palmer." *Colorado Springs Evening Telegraph*, Woman's Edition, December 31, 1894.

"Mrs. William J. Palmer" [obituary]. *Colorado Springs Gazette and Telegraph*, January 3, 1895.

New York Post, November 15, 1870. Courtesy of the New York Historical Society.

Nicolsen, Nigel. *Ightham Mote*. Great Britain: Centurion Press for National Trust Enterprises Ltd, 1998.

Second Biennial Report of the Superintendent of Public Instruction of the Territory of Colorado, for the Two Years Ending Sept. 30, 1873. Denver, CO: Wm. N. Byers, Public Printer 1874G.

Sprague, Marshall. *Colorado*. New York: W.W. Norton & Company, 1976.

———. *Newport in the Rockies*. Chicago: Sage Books, 1961.

Thornton, F. C. "Mrs. Palmer Big Factor in Early Days." *Colorado Springs Sunday Gazette and Telegraph*, August 1, 1926.

———. "Mrs. Palmer's Splended Part in City's Building." *Colorado Springs Gazette and Telegraph*, Fifty First Annual Edition, April 8, 1923.

Turpin, Jeanette. *General William J. Palmer*, Colorado Springs, CO, 1924.

Wilcox, Rhoda D. *The Man on the Iron Horse*. Colorado Springs, CO: Denton Printing Co., 1959.

Wolcott, Frances M. *Heritage of Years*. New York: Minton, Balch & Co., 1932.

RECORDS, PERSONAL PAPERS, JOURNALS, AND DIARIES

General William Palmer Collection. Stephen H. Hart Library, Colorado Historical Society. Denver, CO.

Marriages Taken from the New York Evening Post, *1863–1874*. New York Public Library. New York, NY.

William Jackson Palmer Collection, Timothy Nicholson Collection, and Elsie Queen Nicholson Collection. Colorado Springs Pioneers Museum, Starsmore Center for Local History. Colorado Springs, CO.

Vital Statistics. Kentucky Historical Society Library.